D0871308

Fletcher Martin

H. LESTER COOKE, JR.

HARRY N. ABRAMS, INC., PUBLISHERS, NEW YORK

1. FRONTISPIECE. Fletcher Martin working. Photograph by Peter Jones

Library of Congress Cataloging in Publication Data
Martin, Fletcher, 1904–
    Fletcher Martin.

    Bibliography: p.
    Includes index.
    1. Martin, Fletcher, 1904–   I. Cooke, Hereward
Lester.
ND237.M247C66   759.13   75-2472
ISBN 0-8109-0319-9

Library of Congress Catalogue Card Number: 75-2472
Published by Harry N. Abrams, Incorporated, New York, 1977
All rights reserved. No part of the contents of this book may be
reproduced without the written permission of the publishers
Printed and bound in Japan

CONTENTS

LIST OF PLATES

*Colorplates are marked with an asterisk**

Fletcher Martin

Art historical studies indicate that five factors determine what an artist produces, whether he be a fifteenth-century Italian or a twentieth-century American. The first is his cultural heritage, that cradle of thoughts, beliefs, ideals, and taboos in which he was raised. The second is his personality, in part an outgrowth of that cultural heritage. A painter may try to disguise his inner thoughts, fears, lusts, and loves, but invariably these are revealed. The third component is the record of his life. Those joys, sorrows, frustrations, and accidents which befall a man leave an imprint on what he produces and how he thinks. The medieval Chinese were the first to realize that a painter, regardless of his era, gives a miniature autobiography, a record of thoughts, moods, and character with each brushstroke. The fourth factor is his training, for a pupil inevitably reflects the work of the master under whom he has trained. Although he may rebel, he nevertheless reflects this training in the very nature of his rebellion. Finally, his technique must be taken into account, since an artist using bent wire will produce a totally different kind of art than if he were using pastel. In addition, technique frequently determines what kind of expression will emerge. For example, the painter Antonio Burri, while imprisoned in a concentration camp during World War II, had only pieces of burlap and occasionally a tattered shirt to work with. He tacked, nailed, and plastered

11

these poor fragments onto boards, creating both a powerful and perfectly valid art form. This obviously is an extreme case, but the fact remains that to understand an artist's work one must understand the potentialities of his tools and methods.

And so we approach the work of Fletcher Martin. Some believe that an artist is a philosopher who reveals his thoughts with paintbrush in hand and that we need inspect only his paintings to learn everything he has to say—that words are unnecessary and only confuse rather than explicate. This may be true. If the reader concurs, he should immediately proceed through the reproductions which span almost all of Fletcher Martin's career. There he will observe the life of a gifted painter and will perhaps learn more than volumes of words can explain.

However, most people tend to understand art better with the aid of a text. For this reason we will provide a verbal setting for the paintings and drawings, hoping thereby to augment the reader's perception and enjoyment. In such an endeavor the art historian is usually dependent upon information culled from the memories of friends, faded letters, and newspaper clippings. Fortunately Fletcher Martin, having escaped the fate of so many artists who achieve fame only after death, has been able to make available the facts of his life, particularly those which he considers most important in his development as an artist.

As we have said, the first fact which determines the cast of any artist's work is his cultural heritage. Fletcher Martin comes of true pioneer stock. The Martins—of English, Irish, and French descent—landed in America in the 1600s and moved west with the frontier to Illinois, then to Iowa, and from there to Colorado. Clinton Martin, Fletcher's father, was heading even farther, into the Klondike, when in Leadville, Colorado, he found the challenge he had been seeking. He returned to Iowa, married his sweetheart, and returned with her to Leadville, where he started his first newspaper. A few years and several moves later, Martin Sr. bought the *Palisade Tribune,* a paper in Palisade, Colorado, a town with a population of about three hundred. It was there, on April 29, 1904, that Fletcher Martin was born, the third child and first boy in a family which eventually included seven children, three boys and four girls, each born two years apart.

A photograph of the main and only street in Palisade in the year of Fletcher's birth (plate 3) speaks eloquently of the time and place. A dusty street lined with false-front stores—a livery stable, saloon, and hotel—leads to a sloping plain at the foot of nearby Grand Mesa. Buggies, wagons, saddle horses, and a few bicycles line the street. Pedestrians casually jaywalk, safe except for the occasional runaway team. The photograph recalls a grade-B Western movie set, but in fact there is nothing false about this picture of Palisade; it was the Western frontier, only a generation removed from the Indian wars.

In 1910 the Martin family moved to Emmett, Idaho, another cluster of ranchers'

2. *High, Wide, and Handsome*. 1953.
Lithograph, 15×11″.
Associated American Artists, New York

3.   ABOVE. Street scene in Palisade, Colorado, the artist's birthplace. Photograph, 1905

4.   RIGHT. Fletcher Martin at the age of four. Photograph

5.   FAR RIGHT. The house in which Fletcher Martin was born, Palisade, Colorado. Photograph

homes on the frontier. Fletcher's father, of whom the artist speaks with both awe and respect, tinged with some very painful memories of chastisement, followed the pattern of his previous enterprises by purchasing the *Emmett Index,* an ailing local newspaper with a circulation of just a few hundred. The paper, hand-set and printed on a hand-fed, drum-type press, was a family business, every member having an assigned task. Usually the only outsider was the typesetter, often a hobo printer, a professional belonging to a now extinct species. Fletcher recalls that typesetters just off the freight train would appear without warning—hungry, craving a drink, and ready for work. They rarely stayed longer than a week or so before disappearing as mysteriously as they had arrived. Fletcher was fascinated with this drifting race of itinerant craftsmen, with their stories of adventures, their lore and varied experiences—experiences he would someday share.

As his next venture in those days of land grants and unfenced prairies stretching to the horizon, Martin Sr. bought several hundred acres of sagebrush-covered ranch land just north of Emmett. The family moved to their new domain in a covered wagon and set up house in a tent near the corner marker of their land. With the help of neighbors they built their house and barn. Fletcher was six years old and ready to begin his formal education. However, there was no school. At that time and place in American history, schooling, like everything else, was a matter of private enterprise. Martin Sr. and friends from neighboring ranches built their own schoolhouse, complete with bell, playground, and outhouses. When the school opened, the Martin children represented one-third of the student body, ages six to seventeen. The teacher, a young man from the East, conducted all grades more or less simultaneously.

Art in a frontier town such as Emmett was virtually nonexistent, consisting as it did of posters advertising a circus, and black-and-white newspaper advertisements extolling the virtues of farm machinery, Ford motor cars, or Lucky Strike cigarettes. Fletcher remembers that his first exposure to any form of "fine art" was through a classmate who drew battle scenes depicting bloody encounters between Indians and cowboys in the hills only a stone's throw away from the school. Young Martin was greatly intrigued by the magic skill of this friend who brought to life scenes which were within living memory of the older ranchers in the area. Following this example, Martin began his career as an artist by drawing similar scenes of savage battles.

This introduction to art, rudimentary to say the least, had, nonetheless, a lasting influence upon Martin's conception of the creative process. Recalling the experience in a 1968 catalogue for the Roberson Center for the Arts and Sciences, Martin wrote: "It seems to me that the stimulation and motivation for my painting today is not unlike it was in my youth—though more discriminating, I hope, and less

6.   The district school attended by Fletcher Martin (third from the right, front row) while living on the ranch near Emmett, Idaho. Photograph, 1914

concerned with content. It is both a vision and the result of visual experience. The drawings I made as a child were fantasies on a theme, and so, in essence, are all my paintings, with few exceptions. . . . They are all inventions."[1]

With this awakening interest in art, Martin spent whatever time he could sketching inventive compositions. But life on the frontier left precious little leisure time. Ranching was a hazardous undertaking at best, demanding backbreaking work by all and, in equal part, very good luck. For several years the Martin farm prospered with its orchards, fields of alfalfa, horses, and cattle. Then came bad crop years and the ranch "went broke" leaving them with no alternative but to pull up stakes and move on once again. Fletcher Martin became acquainted early with the bitterness of failure and with the determination necessary to begin again. Both became keynotes of his personality and may account in part for his early maturity, both as a man and as an artist. The writer William Saroyan, who became a close friend of Martin when the artist was in his twenties, recalls that even then, "the thing that is memorable about him was a quality of quietude. He seemed to be at home in the world. There was a touch of melancholy in him. He spoke slowly and in a deep voice. He seemed to move with a pace that was his own. Everybody else I was apt to meet in those days seemed to be in a hurry. He wasn't. One sensed in his nature the strength of a sensitive and gentle personality."[2]

The Martin family moved from their ranch to Kamiah, a village on the Nez Percé Indian reservation at the foot of the Bitteroot Range. Black mountains frowned on the settlement from the east, to the west a canyon valley flanked the Camas Prairie. The teepee village of the Nez Percé Indians was a short distance away on the alluvial plain. Arriving with only his good name and experience, Martin Sr. was somehow able to borrow enough money to buy yet another ailing newspaper, the *Kamiah Progress,* with a circulation of four hundred. Thus the Martin family was again in the printing business, the children working every day after school and all day Saturday. Although denied many of the carefree hours of a normal childhood, Fletcher acquired training vital for his future by becoming an expert printer, having learned every phase of the trade at first hand.

In the era before television and the movies, the town of Kamiah, like Emmett, offered few diversions. The principal entertainments were local parades and visiting rodeos. The Kamiah Indian Band, consisting of Indians and white settlers, founded and led by Martin Sr., was costumed in authentic Nez Percé war bonnets and buckskins. Parading through the streets, its bright array and theatrical flair contrasted strongly with the harshness and drudgery of everyday frontier life. And the rodeo riders, willingly facing danger and even death to provide a spectacle for the entertainment of their audience, contributed to Fletcher's vision of the world as a stage upon which the human drama plays itself out. Although never blatantly expressed, this attitude may be detected in the frequently heightened emotion radiating from his images of intense physical action (plates 120, 145) or from dazzlingly complex design structures (plates 88, 90).

In Kamiah Martin also saw his first professional artist, an itinerant "primitive" painter who drifted into town and set up business in the local barbershop. This marvelous visitor amazed the townspeople as he mixed his pots of paint—one the color of the skies, another of green grass, one recalling the hills, another the color of sand, others suggesting the whiteness of clouds or the shimmering blue of lakes. Then, with what to young Martin seemed incredible wizardry, he moved from panel to panel, conjuring up scenes of deer feeding in the forests, canoes gliding over the azure waters of moonlit lakes, seascapes recalling descriptions of the isle of Capri, or Indians gathering around the campfire under a star-spangled sky. For settlers faced with a life of grinding hardship, these fantasies seemed like visions of a promised land of peace and plenty, and sold briskly at two dollars apiece. Martin watched him day after day, and the hobo artist, with his magical skill and spellbinding tales of exotic places and romantic figures, quickly became Fletcher's beau ideal. Thus stimulated, his growing interest in drawing led Martin to send for a correspondence course in cartooning.

However, he had little time to do more than pay the bill for those lessons. With the advent of World War I the family moved on to Puyallup, Washington, and then to Seattle, where Martin Sr. was employed at *The Seattle Times*. Thirteen-year-old Fletcher sold newspapers briefly before joining Western Show Print, a firm specializing in the production of large, gaudy outdoor posters. As a seven-dollar-a-week "printer's devil," Martin did a wide variety of chores for the artists who designed and cut the big basswood blocks from which the posters were made. When printed, these became eye-catching billboard displays advertising the circus, with troops of pachyderms, trapeze artists of unimaginable beauty and daring, Buffalo Bill and his Indians, racehorses and prize bulls, giants and midgets. While Fletcher was naturally attracted to the carnival atmosphere of these posters, they were also of great value in teaching him about the disposition of large color areas within a linear graphic framework. What he learned from them expanded his knowledge of the possibilities of the print as a vehicle of artistic expression, and later helped him in the solution of problems inherent in the medium of oil.

Although now greatly interested in art, Fletcher Martin at the age of sixteen had not yet been to a single museum or seen a first-rate painting. For him the horizons of the art world still stretched no further than magazine illustrations and the funny papers. Moreover, had Seattle been able to offer such exposure to the fine arts, Fletcher's opportunity to enjoy them would have been brief. His father, whose restless spirit made him unable to tolerate any one place for very long, moved the family to Craigmont, Idaho, another townlet on the frontier, and again purchased a local newspaper. Main Street was a row of fake-fronted wooden shops on either side of a thoroughfare of rutted earth, either hub deep in mud or choked with dust. The prairie wind soughed around the grain elevators at the railroad depot, scorching in summer and chilling to the marrow in winter.

Once more, producing the weekly newspaper was a family affair. The children were now experienced enough to form such an efficient team that their father had time and energy left to enter local politics. He became a public figure of note.

Eventually Fletcher began to kick at the traces. He felt that there was more to life than printer's ink. He worked for the family newspaper without pay, which, according to the standards of the frontier, made him a simpleton. This he would not tolerate. He joined a surveying crew working in the mountains and later put his farming days to good use by driving a mule team and harvesting wheat. He also operated the projector in the local movie house where his sister sold tickets. Finally he ran away from home and lived as a hobo harvesting fruit. He returned home to finish high school, but was asked to leave before graduation, not because of any lack of intelligence, but, according to the unanimous opinion of the staff, because he was an unmanageable nuisance.

Then followed a full year of drifting from one job to another through the Northwest, working in the fields, lumber camps, printshops, and on highway construction jobs. Throughout his travels he sketched incessantly, and although his subjects were usually pornographic ones made to amuse his companions, the act of drawing itself contributed greatly to his subsequent technical skill. His life consisted of flophouses, hobo jungles, and haystacks; he traveled by boxcar, flatcar, tankcar, and on the rods—the horizontal bars beneath freight cars which afford just enough room for a person to lie down and hold on for dear life. His luck, like that of any drifter, was precarious at best. Occasionally the going got rough, but with that pride and determination acquired years earlier, he refused to beg. When asked years later if he ever became desperate, he replied: "None of this was real hardship. Everything was so exciting or potentially so. It was freedom, movement, change, life, color, and drama. Remember Conrad's *Youth*? It was like that, awful but wonderful."[3]

However, during the depths of the 1922 depression Fletcher's luck finally ran out. Living on Skid Row in Portland, Oregon, he roamed the dock area along with hundreds of other men, anxiously scanning the blackboards on which jobs were listed. None was available. During the day he subsisted on the handouts of soup kitchens. At night he drifted with the other men to some flats on the outskirts of the city where underground brick kilns warmed the earth sufficiently to enable sleep. For Martin, then seventeen, the romantic excitement of complete independence was rapidly losing its appeal. He was hungry and tired. Much of the excitement and color must have faded, for a smartly uniformed Navy recruiting officer's guarantee of three square meals a day and a roof over his head prompted Martin to lie about his age and sign up. During the next four years he learned the hard way that discipline in school was one thing and in the service quite a different matter. In his first year he was defendant in a summary court-martial and then in a deck court-martial which resulted in more than fifty hours of extra duty, the loss of five months pay, and a trip to Panama in the brig. During the next three years the record was less troubled. His globe-trotting itinerary reads like an exotic travelogue —Pago Pago, Australia, Hawaii, the Caribbean, and New Zealand. On duty he was a signalman, off duty he was a light-heavyweight boxer in the fleet. His activity as an artist consisted of decorating certificates commissioned by shipmates to celebrate crossing the Equator, documents which Martin claims are now fortunately lost. Despite the limited output, these years provided Martin with a storehouse of memories which he later transferred to canvas. In 1926 he was discharged from the Navy in San Francisco.

Martin started again on the job-hunting trail. In 1925 he had married Cecile Booth, a college classmate of his sister and a talented poetess whose friends included many of the leading contemporary writers. Cecile was a major influence in turning Martin toward more intellectual pursuits. He became a voracious reader, his interests including science, mathematics, philosophy, sociology, and literature. His education was enhanced by frequent discussions with such friends as William Saroyan, Reuben Kadish, Philip Guston, Nathanael West, and Budd Schulberg. It has always been Martin's belief that "if your curiosity is great enough, even about highly specialized professions, you can become educated. Education is like everything else, if you want it very much, you can get it without formal channels."[4]

After brief stints as a laborer at the Fox Hills Studio in Hollywood, as a door-to-door salesman, and as a movie extra, he returned to the job of printer, the only trade he knew well. His boss, Earl Hays, worked for the movie industry producing whatever printed objects were needed, from Civil War newspapers to calling cards. Martin enjoyed the work and remained with Hays for nine years.

Earl Hays was the first to appreciate Martin's talent as both a graphic artist and a painter. Determined to do whatever he could to further Martin's ambitions, he gave the would-be artist as much time off as he wanted to pursue his goal and, with a mixture of generosity and foresight, purchased his first works. Hays's assessment of Martin's potential was fully justified. In 1931, through competition, Martin earned a full-time scholarship at the Stickney School of Art. Although his job with Hays prevented him from accepting the scholarship, he did begin attending the monthly lectures.

Unlike most artists, who spend the greater part of their lives struggling for recog-

7. Fletcher Martin in the US Navy. Photograph, 1924

nition, there are comparatively few years between the time Martin first began to work seriously and public recognition of his work. However, the brevity of this period gives little indication of the enormous efforts it involved. During the day Martin worked in Hays's printshop. At night and on weekends he painted, either in his room or outdoors. Whatever time was left he spent browsing through printshops and bookstores collecting reproductions of great art works. His favorite artists were Signorelli, Giotto, Uccello, Piero della Francesca, Toulouse-Lautrec, and Degas, all of whom were adept in the graphic medium. He also haunted the local galleries and the Los Angeles County Museum of Art. By careful study of both original works and reproductions, Martin taught himself the rudiments of painting and with a keen eye and will to succeed, he accomplished in a few years what other artists often spend a lifetime to achieve.

By the early 1930s he had become an accepted figure in the intellectual circles of Los Angeles, frequenting the studios and homes of the great and near great, avidly absorbing all he could. As he himself expressed it, he attended "Osmosis University" and, after years of night school, graduated magna cum laude. One of the artists who made a great impression on him was the Japanese, Foujita, with whom Martin worked briefly in 1931. Foujita was noted for his blend of a native Japanese feeling for line and a Parisian sensibility for feminine charm, a combination of great interest to the American (plate 8). Foujita and his French wife became Martin's close friends. In the evenings he and Foujita would sit in the garden sketching Foujita's wife. When asked if he had been influenced by Foujita's drawing technique, Martin said, "There might have been a brief period, but only very brief."[5] Admittedly however, a most decisive influence in this early period did come from another artist, a dynamic Mexican who was spending some time in Los Angeles while in exile from his native land.

David Alfaro Siqueiros, whose great gift as an orator and political activist had resulted in a prison sentence and exile, was conducting what he called informal cooperative art classes while executing a mural on Olivera Street in Los Angeles. There students and the master worked together on the project. Martin's account of how he and Siqueiros came to work together provides an interesting sidelight on the climate of opinion in the art world of the thirties:

I saw in the paper that the Mexican painter Siqueiros was giving a talk on dialectical materialism at the John Reed Club. I didn't know what dialectical materialism meant, nor did I know what kind of a place the John Reed Club was, but I did know who Siqueiros was and I was there early to see and hear him. In the lobby of the club was a long table covered with books and pamphlets. Looking them over gave me the answer about what this society was all about. It was Communist. So was Siqueiros, I guess.

8. *Fletcher Martin.* Drawing by Foujita. 1933. Collection the artist

Siqueiros rose to speak in Spanish, with a lady acting as interpreter. He suffered through a couple of her colorless translations, then jumped up and said he would speak in English, which he did with passionate eloquence and an atrocious accent. Soon afterward, he announced that he was accepting students to assist him on a large outdoor fresco on Olivera Street, the original Mexican street in Los Angeles.

Since I had to work all day, I didn't think I could sign up, but I did spend every night down there watching the progress and talking with the Maestro.[6]

Although one would expect that Martin's first exposure to the fresco technique would have prompted his greatest excitement, the artist points to a different aspect of this experience: "His great effect upon me, however, did not come from this [watching Siqueiros work]. It was the powerful impress of his personality. He talked little of art but at length about life and ideas, and one got the feeling that life was delicious and rich and that ideas, poetic ideas, made it so."[7]

Ideas—poetic ideas—quickly became the substance, the life-giving force of Fletcher Martin's paintings. Deeply impressed by Siqueiros's philosophy, Martin abandoned the romantic interest in classical subjects which characterized his first attempts and began to draw upon the wealth of memories which his childhood years and keen eyes had given him. The conceptual process gradually dominated the purely perceptual. A Martin painting is not a mere transcription of nature dependent upon reference to its model. Each is a memory, a recollection of some previous experience. It may be a fleeting visual experience—a gesture, a facial expression, a physical action. Or it may be a life experience—dirt farming, hobo existence, navy life. These memories become distilled into veils of associative mood which both surround and transform the physical forms. Moreover, it is the artist's intention that the timeless or universal qualities thus obtained will prompt spectator participation: "When these other eyes choose to contemplate, they too bring, and they must be allowed to do so, new and personal elements to the composition, making it a living and vital thing."[8]

A Lad from the Fleet (plate 28) is an example of this conceptual process. Painted several years after Martin's naval career ended, it is no realistic portrait of a prizefighting sailor waiting in his corner for the next round to begin; it is Martin's recollection of a man who actually faced him across the ring, enveloped by the daze of combat, trying desperately to regain his strength and determination for the coming round.

Home from the Sea (plate 32) demonstrates Martin's "idea painting" applied to nonfigural compositions. He explains that he had once seen the remains of a boat washed up on the Oregon shore. The vision, probably dating from 1922, gestated for a very long time, in the course of which Martin was prompted to consider the

boat and the sea in terms of human life. The sinister role of nature which he came
to associate with the recollection of that scene became the controlling element
of the design when he finally decided to commit his memory to canvas. The sky
forecasts further storms to batter the already cold and menacing sea. The jagged,
unassailable cliffs in the distance negate any hope of safe landing. The broken figurehead, added last, climaxes the scene of destruction and despair.

Although originating in often highly personal memories and experiences, almost
all of Martin's paintings and drawings are devoid of cloying sentimentality or blatant social commentary. In *A Lad from the Fleet* he is content to recall the image of
a dazed sailor wearied by fighting. Any comments on the brutality of the sport are
those of the spectator, not the artist. So too, in *Tomorrow and Tomorrow* (plate 26),
Martin simply presents us with the image of a prostitute standing at the door, gaz-
ing at a darkened and dismal cityscape while slowly removing her blouse for yet
another "client." The artist has used every design element to express her reluctance,
despondency, and resignation. But the emotional content is generated by the prostitute herself; the artist has not inserted any social commentary on her profession.
Martin approaches virtually every subject objectively yet with a tolerant understanding and obvious affection, achieving a balance between the emotional sterility
of much modern art and the didactic harangues of the Social Realists. This generosity of spirit, this ability to sympathize while never relinquishing control over the
subject, is characteristic of the best of Martin's work.

In the summer of 1932 while traveling through the East, Martin visited Katonah
and Woodstock, N.Y., where he met some of the leading figures in American art of
the time—Alexander Brook, Louis Bouche, Yasuo Kuniyoshi, Peggy Bacon, and
Niles Spencer. These were the artists over whose works Martin had pored in the
many art periodicals he had collected, and he recalls being in "seventh heaven"
upon finding himself actually in their presence. They respected his burning desire
but wondered about his chances considering the economy of the times. In less than
two decades Martin would return to Woodstock, not as an eager young artist but
as a highly respected member of the teaching staff of the Art Students League.

Upon his return to Los Angeles in 1933 Martin had his first one-man show at the
Dalzell Hatfield Galleries, an exhibition of woodcuts which met with considerable
critical success. Determined, however, to become a painter, he immediately resumed
his private studies.

In the following year Martin finally had the opportunity of working with Siqueiros, an opportunity which Martin himself was instrumental in setting up. By
the time the Olivera Street project was completed, Siqueiros was in trouble with
the immigration authorities because his visitor's permit had expired. Exiled from
Mexico, Siqueiros was extremely anxious to obtain some kind of employment which

would keep him in the United States. The opportunity presented itself when Dudley Murphy, a movie director and a friend of Martin, asked him to arrange a meeting with Siqueiros. Murphy claimed that the event was like meeting El Greco or Goya and later casually remarked: "Wouldn't it be great if Siqueiros would do a fresco on the wall in my garden?" Martin conveyed the thought to Siqueiros, who, much to Murphy's surprise, consented to paint the mural for next to nothing if only he and his family could live with Dudley while the wall was being done, his reasoning being that a palatial residence near Malibu would probably be the last place immigration authorities would look for an exiled Mexican Communist artist.[9]

Martin was the official assistant on this project. Every day he left Earl Hays's shop at five in the afternoon and drove the twenty miles to Dudley's house.

Siqueiros would indicate a section for that night. I would mix the mortar and prepare the section. This would take maybe a couple of hours. . . . Usually Siqueiros painted each section himself, but he occasionally would let me develop an unimportant part. He always contended that public murals should be done as a collective effort, but in practice he couldn't stand to have anybody else paint parts that were of any importance to the composition.

He usually painted between midnight and three or four in the morning. Then we would have coffee and eggs and more talk. There was always a sense of elation and accomplishment after the night's work.[10]

The Murphy project took two-and-a-half months to complete. Although the experience was to have its influence reflected in Martin's later murals, he was not to see Siqueiros again for twenty-seven years: The Mexican's politics, with which Martin disagreed, prompted a violent argument and the long interruption of an important friendship. In the meantime, Martin's career advanced with meteoric speed.

In 1934 he had his first one-man exhibition of paintings at the San Diego Fine Arts Gallery, and in the spring of 1935 a one-man show at the Los Angeles County Museum. In the same year, at the Sixteenth Annual Painters and Sculptors Exhibition at the Los Angeles County Museum, Martin's *Rural Family* (plate 9) won both the First Los Angeles Museum Award and the five-hundred-dollar Van Rensselaer Wilbur Prize, a much-coveted honor in view of the fact that Martin was a virtual newcomer to the ranks of American artists.

These early works attest to the fact that even from the outset Fletcher Martin was primarily a classical artist in the sense that his art almost always concerns the human figure. In the sixth century B.C., Greek sculptors carved kouroi, figures of the gods in human form, expressing not only Grecian ideals of physical beauty but also their religious beliefs, hopes, and fears. Since that time the human form has been the pivot around which Western art has revolved. Even in the Middle Ages,

9. *Rural Family.* 1935. Oil on canvas, 48 × 48". Private collection

when man's physical body was generally regarded by theologians as a sinful burden, ideas were expressed in terms of the human form.

Although we accept this concept, usually without second thought, there is the contrasting Oriental philosophy which claims that man is not master of all he surveys, but rather a cog in a vast machine infinitely superior to him and far beyond his control. The Oriental artist spends many years learning to paint the bamboo because this plant, with its willowy grace and infinite variations, symbolizes for him the Creation itself. He is nurtured in the belief that every mood, thought, ideal, and hidden force of the universe can be expressed in terms of the bamboo, not the human body. Laden with snow, silhouetted in the moonlight, whipped by winds, or budding in the spring, the bamboo, not man, crystallizes life and symbolizes the mysterious forces which govern existence. Western man may glimpse these overtones in Oriental art, but it is always the human figure to which he returns as a consequence of his anthropocentric philosophy.

That Fletcher Martin should be firmly in the mainstream of Western thinking is not at all surprising. But his preoccupation with the human form as subject matter goes beyond a mere reflection of race. Several famous Western artists have, after all, been primarily concerned with still lifes, while others have concentrated upon landscapes. To be sure, there are a number of superb still lifes in Martin's oeuvre (plates 84, 174, 175), as well as nonpopulated landscapes (plates 35, 48, 110). Yet the number of such subjects, in comparison with those concerning the human figure, is relatively small. Martin's ideas are usually embodied in the representation of the human body. Even when painting a seascape, he includes a sculptured figurehead as a reference to the existence of man. For him, the Oriental's bamboo is without significance unless held by man.

With his first exhibitions and recognition, Martin began to paint prolifically. In 1936 his name and talent became even more widely known as a result of one-man shows at both the Howard Putzel Gallery in Hollywood and at the Jake Zeitlin Gallery in Los Angeles. Although these early works differ significantly from those of his maturity, they are characterized by that talent for strong design and pictorial organization which is apparent in Martin's paintings from the first.

Design is at the core of Fletcher Martin's art and artistic thinking. Although the word has often come to mean "style" in recent years, "design" is, for Martin, a universal, architectonic principle:

The design is the scaffolding of the picture. It is the trunk and the branches for the foliage and fruit—the foliage and fruit of value and color. Design is the force that maintains order in the composition and conducts the eye through it, revealing unexpected delights for the vision of the spectator. The order which design produces in a composition can be achieved with infinite vari-

ety. There are no rules for it because the invention of a fine design is an important part of the creative act. It can be analyzed after it has been discovered, but that is for the critics to do.[11]

It is important to note that while Martin maintains that design can be analyzed, he also emphasizes that it cannot be codified:

There have been many systems which purport to make the design of a picture a matter of scientific exactitude. These were always academic concepts. Some very inventive artists of today claim to depend upon one of these systems. They say a certain division of the canvas is necessary to achieve an interesting design. In my opinion, the choice of the divisional pattern is very personal and dependent upon the demands of each new problem. A design sense is intuitive.[12]

A painting by Martin may intensely involve the spectator's interest, but he is never truly startled, his perception is never jolted. The experience represented may differ greatly from the spectator's own, but the framework within which the painting exists never departs from his reality. Even in Martin's more abstract designs, such as *The Toss* (plate 118), the figures are not set adrift in a spatially limitless world to which the observer cannot relate. This is true because Martin believes that "the rule or law which cannot be broken is that of balance or equilibrium. A design should never violate these senses in the spectator. No matter how fanciful the concept, the arrangement must not suggest an optical unbalance. Gravity is the foundation of design. The spectator must feel that, should the design structure collapse, it could not fall anywhere but down."[13]

The paintings of the thirties, while early efforts, nevertheless indicate Martin's characteristic simplification of detail, which is always subordinate to the more important functional relationship of each unit to the total organization. This subordination is a component of "composition," a term which Martin distinguishes from design:

The elements of composition embrace the whole creative process. Whatever is brought to final expression on the canvas—large or small, true or false, brilliant or stupid, profound or trivial— these things are elements of the composition; just as the design, the texture, the color, the pattern, and the line are parts of the composition. When these elements have become a picture (and perhaps a work of art), the composition will give it whatever life it has for other eyes.[14]

Exit in Color (plate 30) exemplifies such theories. The bright uninterrupted fence, segregating the darkened grasslands which frame the composition, establishes the layout of the field and focuses attention upon the track, while layered brushstrokes not only define the width and contour of the field but also, through variations of color and highlights, suggest the course's potential for onrushing speed. The horses are sharply highlighted to form increasingly small triangles, the apex of each pointing toward the distance. Their colored blankets complement and augment those recessive brushstrokes which establish the path. Furthermore, these horse blankets, diminishing in color intensity from foreground to background, establish a rhythmic movement of departure accentuated by the ever-decreasing size of the trainers.

Despite its highly calculated construction, the image is a spontaneous interpretation of an experience which the artist had had several days earlier. Indeed, when all of the elements of composition are brought together, the painting has a life of its own for its viewer.

Martin's standard painting procedure has not changed noticeably since the early 1930s. He starts with a very general subject conception, frequently making small, rapid sketches as a means of visual thinking or crystallizing an idea. Unlike many artists, he does not require a long developmental period employing sketches; the concept takes shape rapidly after the idea first occurs to him. Once work on the canvas begins, Martin seldom refers to the sketches again.

He draws on the canvas with vine charcoal, working freely and inventively on the linear design, that all-important skeleton of every Martin painting. The development of this linear substructure generally necessitates many changes from the initial sketches. When the linear design is approximately what he wants, Martin seals the charcoal and prepares the paint. At no time does any part of the canvas achieve finality: "The whole picture is kept constantly alive, and I work all over the canvas every day. The making of a picture should be a creative adventure. The length of time for completion varies greatly. I have done quite successful pictures in several days, and worked weeks on others of the same dimension."[15]

Martin's concepts of design and composition, which not merely permit but actually encourage spectator participation, and his experience of collaborating with Siqueiros made him a perfect candidate for the federally sponsored mural projects of the thirties.

In 1936, Stanton MacDonald-Wright and Lorser Fieleson, in charge of awarding commissions under the Federal Arts Project, decided that Martin was ideally qualified to create a mural in the main auditorium of the North Hollywood High School. This was an enormous opportunity for a painter whose reputation was just beginning to grow. Even though the pay was only ninety-four dollars a month, because he was simultaneously employed in Hays's printshop, Martin was determined to make the most of this opportunity. The true importance of the commission was not financial, but lay in the fact that it gave him a chance to develop and demonstrate his talents. As these federally sponsored projects recede in history, it becomes abundantly clear that they were the single most important factor in giving artists of the thirties the encouragement and public recognition they so desperately needed during the Depression. Without the WPA, the history of American art would probably be vastly different and greatly impoverished.

Martin's initial approach to fresco technique and even, perhaps, the evolution of his monumental conception for the frescoes (since destroyed) in the auditorium of North Hollywood High School may well have been influenced by his experience working with Siqueiros. Siqueiros may also have sharpened Martin's ability to create an almost limitless vision in a somewhat limited space. On the 24-by-12-foot mural on the south wall (plate 18), two colossal figures flanking the auditorium exit (plates 19, 20) seem to support the massive weight of a vast panorama of Indian life, ritual, and belief. To the southwest, seven tribesmen watch from the base of a mountain as the Pleiades, the seven daughters of Atlas and Pleione, are transformed into the seven sister stars of the constellation (plate 21). On the north wall, Indian scouts observe the ascent of Coronado and his treasure-laden men toward "the seven cities of Cibola" represented as an Aztec temple (plate 23). To the northwest, the Indians attack the Spaniards on a mountain slope (plate 22).

Martin firmly rejected Siqueiros's conception of mural painting as an opportunity to advance a political or social ideology. Compared to many by the Mexican artist, the North Hollywood High School murals were largely nonpartisan narrations of past events. Martin also avoided Siqueiros's often brutal facial and figural distortions, employing his brush much as he had his printer's tools, to create a general facial type (plate 24). Similarly, his mural figures were sharply outlined, with interior modeling dependent on the linear contours of stroke rather than tonal modulations (plate 25). Although Martin's innate sense of design and composition enabled him to achieve an impressive integration of mass and movement, he retained the printer's treatment of mountains as flat, linear-faceted shapes and foliage as single brushstrokes of varying concentration.

However, this stylistic analysis—particularly when considered in isolation from the work to which it pertains—can lead too easily to a dismissal rather than a better appreciation of the artist's talents. The limitations noted in Fletcher Martin's style at the age of thirty-two are precisely those which made his auditorium murals so very successful. The representation of historical and mythological subjects without blatant didacticism, the development of basic American types, the graphic clarity of presentation without any loss of compositional intricacy and interest—all are characteristics of a work of art ideally adapted to its setting and audience, in this case the young students of North Hollywood High School.

Martin's first mural project was immediately acclaimed by both professional critics and the public. Almost overnight he became a nationally recognized figure in the art world and was hailed as the rising star of the new generation of painters.

In just a few years, Fletcher Martin's enthusiasm and determination had spurred him on to heights of success and recognition which other artists spend a lifetime trying to achieve. During the next few years his services were in great demand by government-sponsored programs. In 1937 he won the $4900 Award of the Treasury Department's Section of Fine Arts Competition for murals for the Federal Building at San Pedro, California. In 1938 he was selected to create the designs for three 4'6"×12' bas-relief sculptures for the Boundary County Courthouse, Bonners Ferry, Idaho. In the following year he was commissioned to paint a mural for the post office in La Mesa, Texas. During 1940 he painted another, this time for the post office in Kellogg, Idaho, and began a series of twelve mural designs for the Ada County Courthouse in Boise, Idaho. Unfortunately these remained in the cartoon stage, for federal money was beginning to be transferred from art to armaments as America felt the effects of the war in Europe.

While these federally sponsored projects brought Martin's name and talent to the attention of the masses, he was also establishing himself among the art cognoscenti. Between 1938 and 1940 Martin commuted from Idaho, then Texas, then Idaho again to teach drawing at the Art Center School in Los Angeles—an ironic situation for an artist who had never attended a professional school.

In 1939 Martin had his second one-man show at the Los Angeles County Museum. Several months later he participated in an exhibition of California watercolorists at the Riverside Museum in New York City, a show which earned wide critical applause.

Martin's watercolors are primarily on-the-spot field sketches. His early success with watercolors undoubtedly reflects his expertise as a printer, for both mediums employ broad areas of color and demand quick, decisive working practices with little allowance for reworking. A description of the artist at work on a watercolor indicates how at ease he felt with this medium:

First the easel, a three-legged collapsible type showing signs of many years of hard wear-and-tear, is set up with the painting surface lying flat, about three feet from the ground. Martin chooses his subject fast—he knows at once what is and what is not adaptable to his interpretation and spends little time see-sawing between alternate views. He has no objection at all to being observed at work. "Kibitzers" appear from nowhere, and do not seem unwelcome. I have heard Martin talk about dynamite charges with a foreman on a construction site while continuing to work on a half-finished watercolor.[16]

In Martin's oeuvre the watercolor can function as either an independent production or as a shorthand notation to be developed later into a painting on canvas.

In addition to the WPA project in La Mesa, Texas, and the Riverside Museum's exhibition of his watercolors—both of which further enhanced Martin's reputation in the West—the Los Angeles County Museum held another, more extensive one-man show of his paintings and drawings in 1939. *Trouble in Frisco* (plate 27), his recollection of strife among local longshoremen, transformed local commentary into a more universal statement. It was one of his most complex compositions to date and was purchased by the Museum of Modern Art, New York. Martin was also represented in the Los Angeles County Museum's Annual Exhibition of 1939; his painting, *A Lad from the Fleet* (plate 28), was awarded second prize.

Stimulated by the events of 1939, Martin went to New York in 1940 for his first one-man exhibition of paintings and drawings to be held in Manhattan, at the Midtown Galleries. Until then he had been a relatively obscure figure in the Eastern art world despite the presence of his *Trouble in Frisco* at the Museum of Modern Art. The exhibition at the Midtown Galleries received rave reviews, establishing him as a leading member of the American art world. The critics were astute, recognizing Martin as an artist who had arrived at emotionally rich and suggestive statements which never waved the flag despite their origin in the content and quality of American life. The Metropolitan Museum of Art purchased a gouache, *Juliet* (plate 33).

Although Fletcher Martin received much critical acclaim for his nonregionalist paintings, it nevertheless came as a surprise when, in 1940, he was appointed to replace the intensely regionalist Grant Wood as artist-in-residence at the University of Iowa. In the late thirties painters of note tended to become protégés of educational institutions. The artist-in-residence concept was based on the belief that students with creative instincts would profit by mere contact with established artists. The artists, for their part, would have an assured income and thus be freed to use their time creatively.

Grant Wood had been entrenched at the University of Iowa, but long-standing personality conflicts with other members of the Art Department reached an impasse and Martin suddenly received a telegram from the head of the Department asking him to take Wood's place. The situation seemed a bit bizarre to Martin. His professional training had consisted of nine years in a printshop making movie inserts and two-and-a-half months "assisting" Siqueiros. Academically, he had never even graduated high school, much less attended college. Nevertheless, always adventurous, Martin piled everything he owned into an aging station wagon and set out for Iowa with less than one hundred dollars in his pocket. Gambling—the subject of many of his paintings—enabled him to complete the trip richer than when he had started. In due course he was installed in his post, the University Gallery marking the occasion with a one-man exhibition.

The State University appointed him for one year. Upon completion of his duties Martin was made head of the Department of Painting at the Kansas City Art Institute, a post left vacant by the dismissal of Thomas Hart Benton, who, like Grant Wood, clashed with the trustees and the administration. Martin's reputation as both a painter and a romantic figure—the self-taught ex-prize fighter who looked like a pirate of the Spanish Main but painted with great generosity of spirit—made these appointments popular with the students and the public.

However, Fletcher Martin has never regarded himself as a teacher or considered the formal study of art to be a prerequisite for success. While he admits that association with fellow art students provides a stimulation which cannot be duplicated, Martin claims that "it takes a certain natural skill, a creative attitude toward life and a profound, unswerving interest to become an artist. The rewards are abundant but rarely material. There are no obvious inducements as in some other professions."[17] Indeed, although he has taught at many different levels during his professional career, Martin rather doubts the value of an academic approach. Instead he emphasizes that the determined artist finds his own methods and teaches himself:

The use of formulae for design in teaching is a great temptation for many teachers. The educational background of the student usually conditions him to expect some such system—a correct, scientific method for putting a picture together. With a recipe, the student, instead of being at first frustrated and confused, as he should be, feels an almost immediate sense of comprehension and accomplishment. The teacher is in turn comfortable in his authority, because he can apply his rule to some of the greatest masterpieces and refer the skeptic to many impressive texts on the subject. The student, being able to see the logic of the system even before he is able to apply it, respects a teacher with such reasonable ideas.

Unfortunately, this easily understood and assimilated idea is just as unworthy of the creative spirit as the bad painting it will encourage. The logic the student is so accustomed to seek is not a desirable factor here. It will not serve him as an artist nor as a lover of art.[18]

Martin believes that his primary function as a teacher is to maintain, even heighten the sense of excitement which a student feels about his own work. In such an atmosphere the student will educate himself. "The sense of adventure and invention, intuition and untarnished mind's eye," writes Martin, "these are the qualities to encourage in art-interested man. The fine arts may have great riches for the soul of man, but, like any treasures, they are difficult to come by and vary in meaning for each discoverer."[19] It is important to observe here that Martin refers to "the mind's eye" and "the soul of man," not simply to the eyes or sight as the vehicles of artistic discovery.

Martin remained at the Kansas City Art Institute until after the United States entered World War II. In 1943 *Life* decided to commission a number of the country's leading artists to document American activity in the war. Having received a leave of absence from the Art Institute, Martin accepted the assignment, thereby joining a distinguished group of artists which included Mitchell Jamieson, Ogden Pleissner, Paul Sample, Aaron Bohrod, and Peter Hurd.

His first mission was to North Africa in 1943. He sailed for Casablanca in a ninety-ship convoy as a guest of the commanding officer—a marked contrast to his previous naval experience! Moving among the military with ease, understanding the enlisted man's experience at first hand, Fletcher Martin made an ideal war correspondent and artist. He followed the American armies across North Africa to Tunisia for four months, executing over two hundred pen-and-ink drawings and watercolors. The subjects ranged from spectacular battle scenes to sketches of the troops (plate 55), the natives, and the devastation caused by war (plate 53). During slack times or waits for transportation, Martin would make drawings of equipment: trucks, guns, tanks (plate 54), uniforms, divisional insignia, and emblems.

In 1944 he returned to the United States from the North African Theater for a brief rest, during which time he developed several of his sketches into larger oil compositions. Then he accepted another assignment from *Life,* coverage of the Normandy campaign. He arrived in London along with the V-1 rocket barrage and proceeded to follow the armies during the grim fighting in northern France. He returned to England just in time to witness the massive destruction that the V-2 bombs rained down on the city.

As had been his practice in North Africa, Martin filled several notebooks with vivid sketches and jottings of random impressions. The emotional intensity with which he recorded the war and its effects is indicated—although only in part—by the fact that *Life* devoted both the cover and eleven color pages of its 1943 Christmas issue to his work. The wide circulation of these issues made Fletcher Martin's name known to millions who would not ordinarily be conversant with the work of contemporary American artists. In late 1944 Martin's second one-man show at the Midtown Galleries in New York, consisting of these sketches and the documentary paintings developed from them, was, by any standard, an outstanding triumph.

Although naturally pleased by this recognition, in recalling these years Martin's conversation centers not on the wide publicity he received but on the invaluable experience of on-the-spot sketching—the training it provided him and its effect on all his subsequent work, regardless of medium. "Drawing to me," states Martin, "is the most important skill of the artist. Unfortunately, a tendency has grown in the past few years for students to evade its stern discipline. My greatest pleasure is in its practice and use as an instrument of discovery. In my opinion, there have been as many, if not more, important and profound works of art produced as drawings and prints as there have been paintings."[20]

In general, artists sent to cover the war carried cameras because the pace of combat was often too rapid to permit sketching. When Fletcher accepted the assignment from *Life* to cover the African campaign, he was quite anxious about his qualifications for the job. Never having had to work under such intense pressure, he was not even sure he would be able to draw at all in the climate of combat. To insure against failure, he too carried a camera and a more than adequate supply of film. But even before he reached Casablanca, the camera and film were lost. This proved to be a happy accident. "The loss of my camera made me realize that, for the artist, the photographic document is empty and stultifying as a substitute for a sketch. When I go through the material I gathered on a particular trip and pick up any sketch at random, I can feel the weather, smell the smells, hear the sounds that were there when I made it, no matter how long ago. It is real to me because I lived there a little while, maybe a minute, maybe an hour, but intensely."[21]

Martin realized the negative aspects of working with a camera even more when, on the second war trip, he accepted the gift of a Rolleiflex camera from *Life*. The camera made him "lazy and careless." In Africa he had made over two hundred sketches. From this trip he brought back only fifty drawings but many packs of photos. "Of course the time involved was much shorter, but the camera robbed me of the incentive one must have on a trip like that."[22] None of the photographs from this trip could, like the African sketches, immediately and intensely recall the initial experience. They were too explicit, the making of the shot lacking the personal involvement characteristic of the sketching process. "Since that time," says Martin, "the only materials I carry are pens and sketchbooks. If I miss something it is because it didn't cross my field of vision. If I see it, I have it."[23]

Realizing that photography was a valueless tool for the development of his drawings and paintings gave Martin added incentive to sharpen his visual memory:

If it was not possible to make a drawing on the spot, I would record its important qualities on my mind's eye until I could get it down on paper. . . . My hand sharpened as well as my eye and I got so I could make a sketch with the same direct vigor with which we write when we have something to say. By this I mean that the action of drawing did not get between me and the experience, as it had in former times. . . .

The thing I discovered is that what your eye gives you and your heart responds to is all-important and if you can draw it at all you can draw it later. If you don't wallow in the experience with your eyes and your mind and heart you don't know much about it anyway and you can't get with it if you aren't looking. Even the most cursory note does tend to fix the image and help one to that plateau of visual freedom where almost total recall is automatic. It takes practice, and lots of it, of both eye and hand, to free oneself of the tyranny of the subject before you. You must be the master of it and you can only achieve that by knowing it well.[24]

During the many teaching positions which he has subsequently held, Martin has advanced an interesting philosophy of vision—an attitude toward looking at things —-which he evolved from his experiences as a war correspondent. It is of particular interest to eager young artists because it considers skill and craftsmanship as secondary tools which improve only with time. Foremost is the eye:

The arts exploit different senses, but the one we depend upon, and perform for, is the eye. It is my contention that most people, including many artists, do not use their eyes to really see but only to identify objects. Since the material for our work comes from our visual experience and our understanding of the shape and feel of things in the context of our lives, it is very important that our observational eye be keen. In my opinion, the best device for whetting this power is the practice of sketching in the field. The particular sketch may be of no consequence, but it is important that you have had the experience of making it.[25]

Many of Fletcher Martin's own field sketches dating from the war, such as the Moslem mosques in Tunisia, the ancient olive trees, or the harbor at Bizerte, are executed as graphic shorthand notations, with an economy of line characteristic of a highly talented and sensitive draftsman. This linear economy is a reflection of Martin's thorough training as a printmaker as well as his perceptive study of such masters as Toulouse-Lautrec, whose own impressions were recorded with equal graphic succinctness.

It is an indication of the range of Martin's talent that when time permitted, he was able to translate his shorthand notations into elaborately articulated drawings without sacrificing the immediacy and impact expected of war reportage. *The Scream* (plate 59), now in the Metropolitan Museum of Art, New York, is a superb example. The drawing fairly vibrates with the piercing, horror-filled scream of the woman who tries desperately to avoid the sight of reality.

Destruction is, inevitably, the theme of most of the war drawings. In *Flying-Bomb Damage, Hyde Park* (plate 61), the incessant destruction which became a way of life is embodied in the image of police and civilians calmly gathering up the debris of bomb-blasted trees. It is important to note, however, that Martin's drawings and paintings of World War II are not propaganda exercises. In *The Scream* there is no reference to the nationality of the people; this is true also of the police and civilians of *Flying-Bomb Damage*. Nevertheless, the war drawings and paintings cannot be interpreted as objective recordings of contemporary events, for they reflect too clearly that empathy with and affection for all humanity which characterizes Fletcher Martin's personality. Perhaps the quintessential expression of this quality is *Next of Kin* (plate 60), in which the despair and anguish radiate from the canvas as a universal consequence of war, the nationality of the woman being of no importance whatsoever.

Despite Martin's claim that the impact of his sketches was often dissipated when transferred to canvas, critics agree that he has a remarkable ability to make a rapid sketch on a small scale and then develop a larger interpretation at a later date retaining the emotion, action, color, and movement of the original sketch. In this, Martin belongs to the tradition established by such American artists as Winslow Homer, William Glackens, Everett Shinn, and George Luks. Homer and Glackens are particularly important in having established an American tradition of war coverage in which the incidental, leisure moments are considered valid subject matter to illustrate war life. Martin's *The Gamblers* (plate 51) is one of many drawings and paintings in this tradition. His image of a poker game between seven men, several of whom are mutilated for life, is again devoid of sentimentality or mock heroics, but filled with affection and respect for the dignity and courage of man.

In several of the war paintings Martin transcribes his experiences into symbols or emblems rather than narrations. *Faid Pass* (plate 48), with its soldier's grave and wrecked vehicle at the foot of a desolate mountain range, symbolizes the thousands of burials in anonymous fields that the pace of combat necessitated—in marked contrast to the pomp and ceremony of burial at Arlington. In *Boy Picking Flowers* (plate 49), the soldier's simple appreciation of nature's beauty shows the survival of the best of man's instincts amidst the carnage produced by his worst aspects as symbolized by the wrecked truck in the distance. In *Victory* (plate 74), the triumph of nations, symbolized by uplifted bugles and waving flags, is made hollow by the absence of people, an emptiness underscored by the blackened sun.

When Martin transcribed his rapidly executed sketches into full statements on canvas, his innate sense of design asserted itself strongly. His vision of a German bomber attack on Allied shipping in a North African harbor represents the ack-ack tracers as a decorative criss-cross embroidery while a crashing plane appears in the sky as a luminescent flower. Martin's most ambitious and perhaps most impressive combat painting is *Battle of Hill 609* (plate 56), depicting an engagement in Tunisia between German and American scouting parties. This event occurred when a ground mist suddenly lifted and the two platoons found themselves face-to-face across a country road. Although in fact a minor skirmish, Martin elaborated the composition into a panorama recalling his earliest artistic inventions, in which the Indians squared off against the federal troops in the hills behind Kamiah.

Upon completion of his assignment in Normandy and England, Martin returned to the United States, only to find himself once again on assignment for *Life*. Admittedly it was a pleasanter task—an all-expenses-paid trip to Hollywood to paint

10. *Death of Jurgis' Wife*. 1965. Colored inks and watercolor, $22\frac{1}{2} \times 31''$.
From *The Jungle*, published by The Limited Editions Club and The Heritage
Club. Copyright © 1965 by The Cardavon Press, Inc., Avon, Conn.

11. *Lennie and George*. 1969. Brush and pen and ink, $22 \times 17''$.
From *Of Mice and Men*, published by The Limited Editions Club and
The Heritage Club. Copyright © 1970 by The Cardavon Press, Inc., Avon, Conn.

portraits of Yvonne de Carlo, Charles Laughton (plate 70), and Sylvia Sidney (plate 69). The three portraits were adequate, that of Charles Laughton dressed as Captain Kidd being the most interesting. Interestingly, Fletcher Martin has never considered himself a first-rate portrait painter, nor, for that matter, has he ever really been interested in capturing the physical idiosyncrasies of a specific face. Neither caricatures nor formal portraits, the paintings are an uneasy combination of aspects of both. It is a mark of Martin's acute understanding of his own talents that he did not accept such an assignment again.

Where Martin excelled greatly was as an illustrator, particularly in the medium of print. In 1944 George Macy, head of The Limited Editions Club, asked Martin to illustrate a volume of Bret Harte's stories selected by Oscar Lewis and titled *Tales of the Gold Rush*. It was the first of five volumes which Martin would produce for the club. The others were: *Mutiny on the Bounty* by Nordhoff and Hall in 1946; *The Sea Wolf* by Jack London in 1960; *The Jungle* by Upton Sinclair in 1965 (plate 10); and *Of Mice and Men* by John Steinbeck in 1969 (plate 11).

"I enjoyed illustrating these books," he later wrote, "because, although they were in color, they were essentially drawings. Also because I was given complete freedom of choice as to the subject and medium. . . . This privilege was given me because of my history as a printer."[26] Trained as a printer, Martin knew precisely both the limitations and the potentialities of his medium—black-and-white and colored drawings. His illustrations of Bret Harte's work are acutely in tune with the text. In *The Sea Wolf* his illustrations are again the interpretation of a kindred spirit. His drawings for *Of Mice and Men* are autobiographical—only someone who rode the rails as a hobo, slept on moldy straw in a bunkhouse, or had felt the sting of social injustice could possibly have created a pictorial authenticity equal to that of Steinbeck's text.

In 1945 Martin left the West Coast to settle in New York, where he executed a series of views of that city for the Nathan M. Ohrbach Collection. In the following year, after completing his assignment for The Limited Editions Club, he moved from New York City to the artist's colony of Woodstock, N.Y. Although he had hoped to settle down, the publicity resulting from his war coverage made Martin an artist in great demand for documentary projects, and in 1946 he found himself on the road once again, painting scenes of the rivers of Missouri on a commission for the Scruggs-Vandervoort-Barney Collection (plate 66). This assignment was followed in 1947 by a series for the Gimbel-Pennsylvania Art Collection depicting the anthracite mines in Wilkes Barre, Pa. (plates 67, 68).

In 1947 Martin finally built a permanent residence and studio on Overlook Mountain in Woodstock, where for the next two years he taught at the Art Students League. During this period his reputation in the art world increased greatly. In 1947 *Dancer Dressing* (plate 47) was awarded the prestigious Walter Lippincott Prize for figure painting at the Pennsylvania Academy of Fine Arts. In 1949 *Cherry Twice* (plate 64), a double-image portrait of the artist Herman Cherry, was honored with the Altman Prize of the National Academy of Design.

At the same time Martin's private life was also marked by success. A new marriage which resulted in the birth of two sons provided the artist with a new-found stability and domesticity. This change was inevitably reflected in his work, most notably in his treatment of the female figure.

If there is a leitmotiv in Martin's work, it is the nude or seminude figure. Throughout his life, he has returned more often to this theme than to any other, considering the nude to be "the most challenging and difficult problem for the artist." Almost always the model is a woman, and almost always she is young and beautiful. One looks in vain for any spark of awareness among his models. Like Boucher's in the eighteenth century, Martin's women are delectable abstract shapes, differing in measurements but essentially the same in the message they give. They show no guilt and only rarely any intellectual activity. Nor is there an overemphasis on sensuality. The tuft of hair or hidden crease of flesh, as in Pascin's work, or the suggestive smile of a Fragonard woman are not in Martin's repertoire. His ladies are frankly nonvirginal but seem to be posing in a trance (plate 47). Occasionally they become tinted statues. If there is any emotion, it is conveyed with a gesture rather than an expression (plate 50). One looks in vain for any flash of response in the lowered eyes and noncommittal expression.

After the war Martin's art evolved new forms. The human figure remained the focal point of his painting, but the dramatis personae changed. The women are no longer pagan, day-dreaming feline goddesses in sultry settings. Beginning in the 1950s they become domesticated (plate 80). Children romp around (plate 106), and the mood becomes more lighthearted, the colors brighter, more bouyant. When asked about these changes, Martin said: "We were often on the beach. The sun was bright. It was a sort of holiday and the children were just there."[27] However, one suspects that in these changes there does exists a reflection of Martin's more serene personal life and of the satisfaction derived from the success of his thriving career.

In 1949 Martin and his family moved to the University of Florida where for two years he held the position of Visiting Artist and had another one-man exhibition. Martin's "visiting" was intermittent, to say the least. Almost immediately upon arrival in Florida he accepted a commission from the Lucky Strike Cigarette Company to travel throughout North Carolina documenting the production of tobacco. Then in 1950, along with the artists Edward Chavez, Edward Millman, and Frede Vidar, Martin traveled more than twenty thousand miles on assignment for the Abbott Laboratories which had commissioned the four artists to paint a documentary record of health conditions among the Eskimos of Alaska and the Indians on thirteen United States reservations. With absolute honesty and integrity Martin showed those conditions in all their often ugly reality, his contribution to the project earning him the Merit Award of the Art Directors Club of Chicago.

Throughout the following years he was in constant demand as a teacher, his paintings and drawings incessantly requested for both one-man and group exhibitions. Yet interestingly, despite the enormous attention which he devoted to his students and the huge time-consuming aspects of assembling exhibitions, Martin made his own greatest technical and aesthetic advancements during these very years. He has always believed that great art is far more than the transposition, however accurate or clever, of an image in nature to the two-dimensional surface of a canvas. "You can get the image," he has said, "something that resembles the subject, in fifteen minutes. The final quality of the painting is the sum of many decisions. It is the addition of all the small refinements that give the picture its quality."[28] Martin has never stopped searching for those refinements.

In the late 1940s and throughout the 1950s color took on far greater importance for Martin than it had previously had. The artist recalls that his interest in a more

12. *Don and Clint*. 1957. Charcoal and chalk, 25 × 18″. Collection the artist

extensive palette at this time was motivated by the "simple" recognition that he had not previously fully explored the potentialities of color. In the 1930s and early 1940s his work had tended to be either monochromatic or very limited in hue. The more recent canvases were higher in key. Working with a brighter, more intense palette became a process of discovery, an evolution, sensed but never planned. In the past ten or twelve years Martin has become very interested in even brighter colors linked by even more subtle transitions.

Martin's basic palette consists of Mars black, cadmium red light, cadmium orange, alizarin crimson, olive green, viridian green, cobalt blue, cerulean blue, ultramarine blue, raw sienna, burnt sienna, yellow ocher, cadmium yellow, raw umber, and burnt umber.

Although he rarely uses glazing as such, the color is usually built of many layers of paint which in fact have a certain transparency. Over the charcoal sketch the main color areas are blocked out in shades of gray. The medium is always lean, so that drying is rapid. Copal varnish medium is sometimes used to produce a tacky surface. Occasionally the oil surface is "stroked" with pastels and charcoal, thereby introducing yet another surface texture. Over the monochrome underpainting, color is superimposed in pale, tentative "skins"—cool browns, soft pinks, and pale blues —as often with a palette knife as with a brush.

In the early stages of a painting the emphasis is not so much on specific colors as on the balance and harmony of warm versus cool. This sets up problems in color relationships—when any one color is changed, it affects every other color area in the painting. Some, therefore, must be changed to bring the picture back into harmony. A canvas is apt to be repainted, altered, and transfigured several times. Soon after it has been begun, the work acquires a personality, independence, and growth pattern of its own. It enters into a dialogue with its creator, in a sense leading him into unexpected, infinitely subtle, and often exciting harmonies which he might never have planned or envisioned. These chain reactions have to be looked at long and carefully before their significance can be understood. In fact, Martin's paintings have a sensuous appeal of paint surface which is rarely obvious at first sight.

The extensive observation required to appreciate this sensuous paint surface is partly due to its complete integration with the design structure. Since, as the artist has explained, a successful painting is one in which all elements are harmoniously balanced, the surface which Martin developed in the early 1950s is, to a large degree, a necessary and ultimate result of that wide variety of brushstrokes which the artist employs. Martin's repertoire of brushstrokes ranges from a highly fluid, curvilinear style (plate 162) to a rough, spiky mode (plate 102). The latter style results from the fact that when working with inks or watercolors, he often holds his brush or pen the way a mason holds a trowel—a practice perhaps originating in his

13. *Nude with Hat and Gloves*. 1963.
Watercolor, 24×18″.
Collection Mr. and Mrs. Joseph S. Wohl,
Lawrence, N.Y.

frequent use of a palette knife. In such a position, wrist action is largely an abrupt movement left or right, up or down, rather than a continuous rotation. Martin's brushwork is rapid and decisive, rather like swordplay. He rarely erases or covers his work, showing a self-assurance that undoubtedly dates from his years as a printer (plate 83). Always striving for total artistic integration, Martin at this time began to unite his newly developed harmonies of color blocks with the linear element. His solutions to this problem of total union are varied and complex, contributing to that necessity of extensive observation. The interplay of warm color harmonies and graceful, fluid lines often intensifies the lushness of the tonal relationships while in other cases the deliberate combination of cool harmonies and graceful lines establishes a sensed opposition which makes the work all the more compelling. Moreover, color may function either to soften the thrust of spiky lines (plate 95) or to heighten its dynamic tension (plate 164). Brushwork in combination with color lends a tapestry-like pattern to the design, the overall strength of execution creating a powerful statement out of what in less skilled hands might have dissipated into a too quaint, too charming image (plate 106).

During the fifties and sixties there appears in Martin's work an ever-increasing sense of patternization. Although the human form remains his primary subject, he is more concerned with emphasizing the outline or silhouette than with establishing a sense of three-dimensionality (plate 149). So, too, when he turns his attention to still life, the objects are more diagrammatic than space-displacing (plate 175). As the artist has said: "Although art springs from nature, the artist is the interpreter, not the imitator. The forms of nature are so diverse that there is no symbol of color or shape whose counterpart cannot be found. This decade has seen a real evolution in the attitude of the artist. Though we cannot be sure where painting is going, it seems possible that in the future the abstract synthesis of nature will probably be the most significant form."[29]

14.   *Girl with Plant.* Brush and India ink, 18 × 24″. Collection the artist

Since mid-century, Martin has been involved in an intense search for those abstract shapes and interlocking rhythms of line and color which best convey his many moods and expressions. This interest has not in any way limited his range of subjects. It applies to industrial machines (plate 89), the sights of his beloved Mexico (plate 110), where he has had a home since 1970, the carnival (plate 90), and, most effectively, to dance subjects (plate 91). In *Country Dance,* for example, the composition is threaded together by the linkage of arms and the striped floorboard which create continuous lines of interlocking echoes and recollections. The pattern on the surface plane itself captures the beat and cadence of figures in motion.

"Pattern *on the surface plane*" is of vital importance to Fletcher Martin. The artist claims that from his earliest attempts he has always worked to maintain the surface plane. While striving to develop as rich a patterning as possible, he insists that "the surface plane should never be negated." Martin cites his early experiences working in fresco as a possible source for this predilection.

Although interested in pattern and the two-dimensional reality of the canvas, it must be remembered that Martin has always derived his artistic stimulation from experiences grounded in everyday life. As such, the degree to which his visions can be abstracted for the sake of patternization is somewhat predetermined. His sea birds may be flattened into cardboard cutouts (plate 86) and his clouds reduced to putty-like pancakes (plate 110), but their specific shape identity is never entirely sacrificed. Unlike so many of his contemporaries of the 1940s and 1950s Martin could never be considered an Abstractionist. He does have a portfolio of purely abstract compositions but he refuses to consider these as valid works to which he would return for elaboration and public exhibition. "Abstract painting," states Martin, "is just not my thing."[30] *Evening Nude* (plate 114) typifies the extent of the artist's distillation of reality.

In 1955 Martin won the Gold Medal of the New York Art Directors Club for a work commissioned by *Woman's Day*, that of a fallen jockey being trampled by oncoming race horses. Although sporting pictures had interested the artist from his earliest days in Hollywood, when he and William Saroyan would regularly attend the Friday night boxing matches, it was in the 1950s that Martin acquired increased public attention and critical acclaim for this subject. Among those commissioning sporting paintings was *Sports Illustrated*, for which Martin executed *Victor's Dressing Room*. As a former boxer himself, Fletcher's interest in and identification with that sport has always been great, but he has also depicted football (plate 145), baseball (plate 125), the previously mentioned horse racing (plate 123), and bullfighting (plate 120), an appreciation of which he acquired during his many trips to Mexico. Sporting events give Martin an opportunity to depict men in motion, and the split second when a man devotes all of his mental and physical efforts toward a single goal. Winning or losing rarely interests him. True, Martin can depict a poignant moment of defeat (plate 75), but such instances are few. Success in the boxing ring or death in the arena represent neither victory nor defeat but simply the end of a physical act. This interest in physical action itself, not the advancement of some social comment, enabled Martin to equate athletic movement with the ballet (plate 76) well in advance of the current cinematic practice of filming the rough-and-tumble of football action as a dance in slow motion.

Fletcher Martin considers his paintings of the 1960s and early 1970s to be the best of his career, although the subjects have not changed substantially over the years. Nor can the stylistic transformations be regarded as truly radical, particularly when compared with techniques employed by other artists during the same

15.   *Girl with Violin.* 1970. Pen and ink on rice paper, 12×16″. Collection the artist

16.   *Self-Portrait*. 1969. Pen and ink, 16 × 12″.
Collection the artist

decades. Yet his assessment does have validity. Martin's latest works are genuinely characterized by that "sum of all the small refinements" which, according to the artist, lend any art work its "quality." Those many but subtle refinements endow his paintings of recent years with an even less anecdotal, more universal aspect than had marked his previous efforts. The females of the earlier paintings were generally bathers or exotic nudes. In the later works they are primarily studies of the human figure per se. True, one may perhaps see the beginning of this interest in the human figure as early as 1935, when in *A Lad from the Fleet* Martin painted the image of an archetypal opponent, not a specific portrait. However, this work must still be considered among his sporting pictures. Only in recent years has he developed the human figure truly divorced from its momentary activity and assuming more universal significance. In this respect, it is interesting that when asked recently to list his favorite writers and themes, Martin replied: "He [Conrad] has impressed me for forty years. I like his themes and his style. But do I like him better than Hemingway, Malraux, Graves, Maugham, or Steinbeck? I'm not sure. And this is to say nothing of all the great writers of the past. Shakespeare makes bums of them all."[31] His response to the question is illuminating not only because it shows the scope of his self-education but, more important, because he chose those specific writers who made their primary concern situations, problems, and emotions of a universal nature.

Although a graphic artist from youth, the works of the 1960s and 1970s show an increased graphic dexterity, variety, and versatility characterizing this as his finest period. Moreover, the interior modeling during these years indicates a new synthesis of drawing and painting, once seemingly at odds in Martin's work. In addition, while he maintains the surface plane, Martin has finally resolved a problem on which he had begun to work during the 1950s—the tonal relationships between figure and surrounding canvas.

17.   Study for *The Charge*. 1965.
Pen and ink, 23¼ × 16½″.
Collection Mrs. Alvin L. Chambers, Jr.,
Dayton, Ohio

NOTES

1. Fletcher Martin, *Fletcher Martin: A Thirty Year Retrospective,* Roberson Center for the Arts and Sciences (Binghamton, 1968), pp. 8–9.

2. William Saroyan, "Fletcher Martin," *Art Digest,* vol. 29, no. 3 (November 1, 1954), p. 11. Reprinted in *Fletcher Martin* by Barbara Ebersole (Gainesville, 1954), pp. i–xix (quotation on p. xiii).

3. In conversation with the author, April, 1970.

4. Barbara Ebersole, *Fletcher Martin* (Gainesville, 1954), p. 17.

5. In conversation with the author, March, 1971.

6. Letter from Martin to the author, January 17, 1970.

7. Barbara Ebersole, *Fletcher Martin,* pp. 23–24.

8. Fletcher Martin, "Composition," *The Art of the Artist: Theory and Techniques of Art by the Artists Themselves* (New York, 1951), pp. 40–41.

9. In conversation with the author, September, 1971.

10. Letter from Martin to the author, July 18, 1969.

11. Fletcher Martin, "Composition," *The Art of the Artist,* p. 41.

12. Ibid.

13. Ibid.

14. Ibid., p. 40.

15. Ibid., p. 42.

16. Firsthand observation by the author.

17. Barbara Ebersole, *Fletcher Martin,* p. 33.

18. Fletcher Martin, "Composition," *The Art of the Artist,* p. 41.

19. Ibid., pp. 41–42.

20. Ibid., p. 42.

21. Fletcher Martin, "The Eye Is Your Camera," *Famous Artists Magazine,* vol. 6, no. 2 (Winter 1957), p. 8.

22. Ibid., p. 9.

23. Ibid.

24. Ibid., p. 8.

25. Ibid., p. 6.

26. In conversation with the author, March, 1971.

27. In conversation with the author, June, 1970.

28. Barbara Ebersole, *Fletcher Martin,* p. 51.

29. Ibid., p. 53.

30. In conversation with the author, October, 1970.

31. Letter from Martin to the author, February 21, 1971.

PLATES

18. *Legends of the California Indians.*
1936. Fresco, 24′ × 12′.
North Hollywood High School Auditorium,
southwest corner

19. *Giant in the Earth*. Portion of
Legends of the California Indians.
South wall, left,
in North Hollywood High School

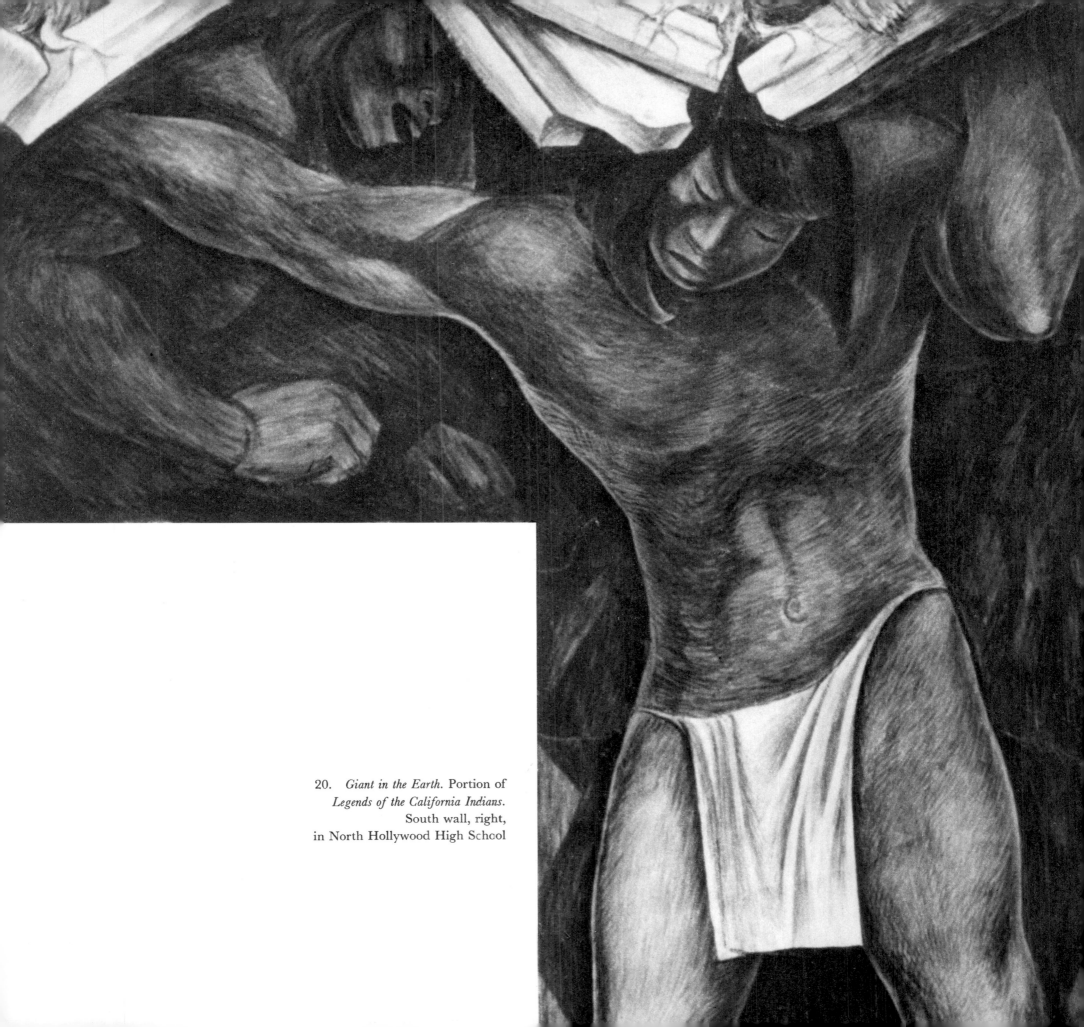

20. *Giant in the Earth.* Portion of
Legends of the California Indians.
South wall, right,
in North Hollywood High School

21. *Origin of the Pleiades.*
1936. Fresco. Detail of
west wall, left, in
North Hollywood High School

22. *Skirmish on the Trail.*
1936. Egg tempera. Detail of
west wall, right, in
North Hollywood High School

23. *Coronado's Journey*. 1936.
Egg tempera on plaster, 24′×12′.
North Hollywood High School Auditorium,
northwest corner

24. *Warrior*. 1936.
Fresco. Detail of west wall, left,
in North Hollywood High School

25. *War Party*. 1936. Egg tempera.
Detail of north wall to right of door,
in North Hollywood High School

26. *Tomorrow and Tomorrow.* 1939.
Oil on canvas, 48 × 30″.
Carleton College, Northfield, Minn.

27. *Trouble in Frisco*. 1938. Oil on canvas, 30 × 36″. Museum of Modern Art, New York. Abby Aldrich Rockefeller Fund, 1939

28. *A Lad from the Fleet*. 1935.
Oil on canvas, 48×30″.
Collection Mike Manuche, New York

29. *A Lad from the Fleet*.
Detail of Plate 28

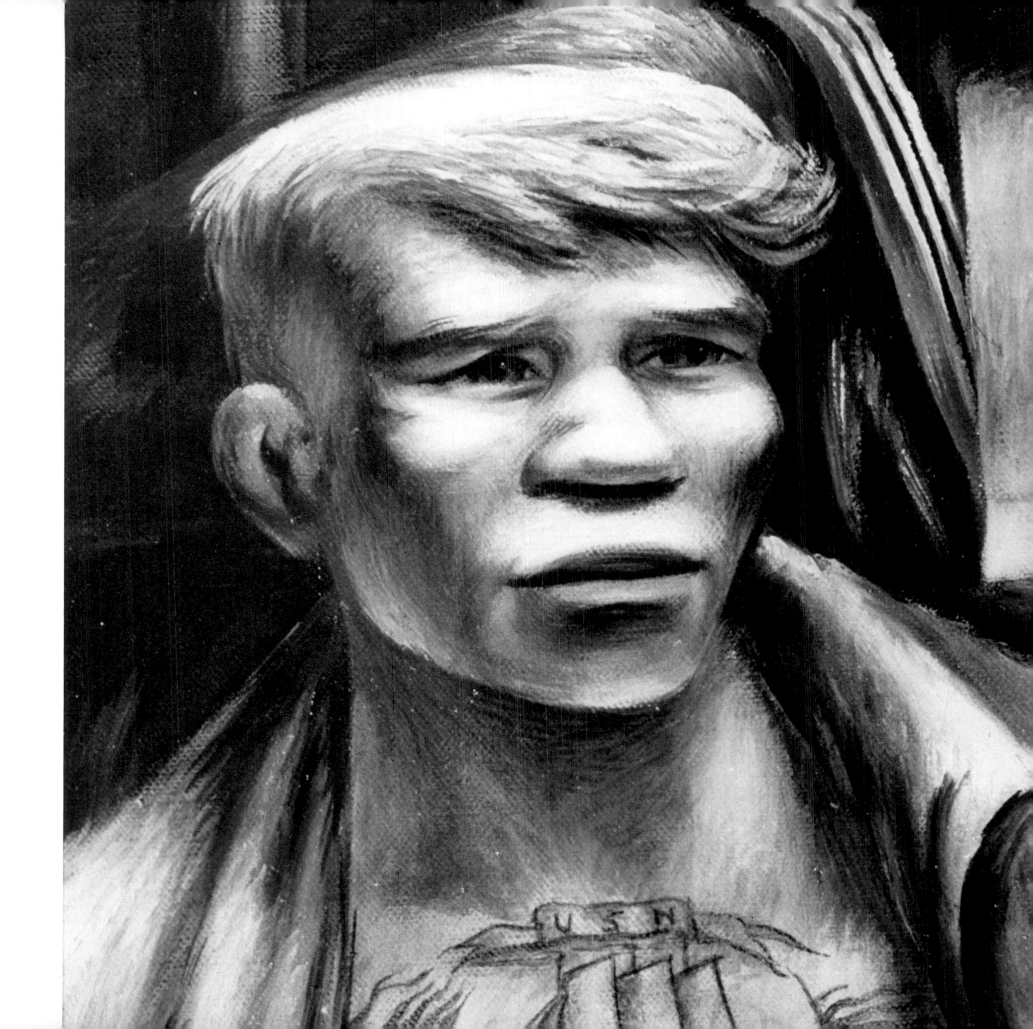

30. *Exit in Color*. 1939.
Oil on canvas, 36 × 30″.
Abbott Laboratories Art Collection,
Chicago

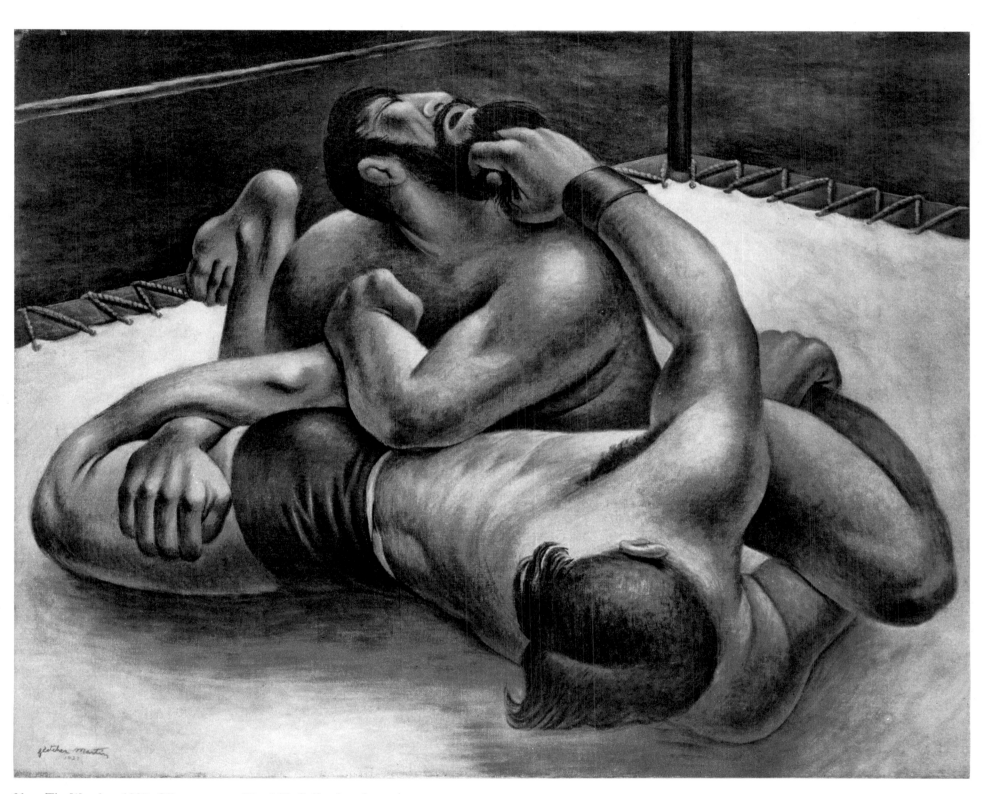

31.   *The Wrestlers*. 1937. Oil on canvas, 26 × 34″. Collection the artist

32. *Home from the Sea.* 1939. Oil on canvas, $35\frac{3}{4} \times 47\frac{7}{8}''$. The University of Iowa Museum of Art, Iowa City

33.　*Juliet*. 1939. Gouache, 18×36″. The Metropolitan Museum of Art, New York. Purchase, 1940, George A. Hearn Fund

34. *Souvenir*. 1941.
Oil on canvas, 36 × 28″.
Collection the artist

35.   *Air Raid*. 1940. Oil on canvas, 26 × 30″. Courtesy of the Los Angeles County Museum of Art, Los Angeles. Gift of Southern California artists

36. *July 4th, 5th, and 6th.* 1940. Oil on canvas, 40×55″. Hirschl & Adler Galleries, New York

37. *Temptation in Tonopah.* 1940.
Oil on canvas, 30 × 20″.
Collection Stanley R. Resor,
New Canaan, Conn.

38. *The Picador*. 1941.
Gouache, 24 × 20″. Collection William Saroyan,
San Francisco

39. *Monica*. 1940.
Oil on canvas, 30×20″.
Private collection

40. *Out at Home*. 1940. Oil on canvas, 20 × 40″. Collection Mike Manuche, New York

41. *Stormy Weather*. 1941.
Oil on canvas, 40 × 24″.
Collection Mr. and Mrs. Benedict Tessler,
Maplewood, N.J.

43. *Lullaby.* 1942. Oil on canvas, 31 × 48″. Collection Mr. and Mrs. Clifford B. West, Blcomfield Hills, Mich.

42. *Lullaby.* Detail of Plate 43

44. *Friend of Man*. 1942. Oil on canvas, 30 × 42″. Collection the artist

45. *Black King*. 1942.
Oil on canvas, $43 \times 25''$.
Collection the artist

46.   *Weeping Girl.* 1941. Oil on canvas, 15 × 30″. Private collection

47. *Dancer Dressing.* 1941.
Oil on canvas, 40 × 24″.
Collection Hollis and Vivian Holbrook,
Gainesville, Fla.

48.   *Faid Pass.* 1943. Oil on canvas, 30 × 36″. Courtesy of the US Army Center of Military History, Washington, D.C. Army Art Collection

49.   *Boy Picking Flowers, Tunisia.* 1943. Oil on canvas, 32 × 28″. Copyright © Time Inc.

50. *Ruby.* 1943.
Oil on canvas, 34 × 18″.
Collection Hollis and Vivian Holbrook,
Gainesville, Fla.

51.   *The Gamblers*. 1943. Oil on canvas, 30×40″. Collection Mr. and Mrs. Peter L. Jacobs, Woodmere, N.Y.

52. *Battlefield: German Graves*. 1943.
Pen and ink, 8×10″. Collection the artist

53. *Across the Inner Harbor, Bizerte*. 1943.
Pen and ink, 8×10″. Collection the artist

54. *Churchill Tank, Cape Bon*. 1943.
Pen and ink, 8×10″. Collection the artist

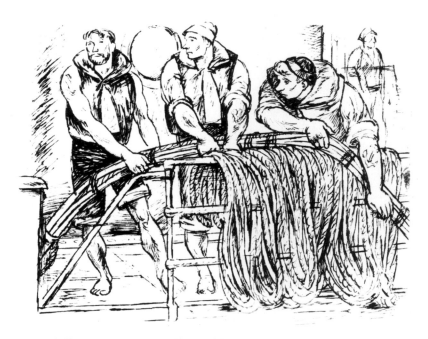

55. *Sailors on the Convoy Oiler*. 1943.
Pen and ink, 8×10″. Collection the artist

56. *Battle of Hill 609*. 1943. Oil on canvas, 30×50″. Copyright © Time Inc.

57. *Survivor*. 1943. Oil on canvas, 30 × 42″. Collection the artist

58. *Killer in Costume*. 1942.
Oil on canvas, 50×36".
Private collection

59.   *The Scream*. 1943. Pen and ink on rag paper, 22×30″. The Metropolitan Museum of Art, New York. Anonymous Gift, 1945

60. *Next of Kin.* 1944.
Oil on canvas, 35 × 24″.
Private collection

61. *Flying-Bomb Damage, Hyde Park.* 1944. Pen and ink, $11 \times 15\frac{1}{2}''$. Collection the artist

62. *Subway Sleepers, London*. 1944. Oil on canvas, 24 × 36″. Collection the artist

63.   *Night Music.* 1945. Oil on canvas, 30×48″. Collection Mr. and Mrs. Richard S. Lembeck, Lawrence, N.Y.

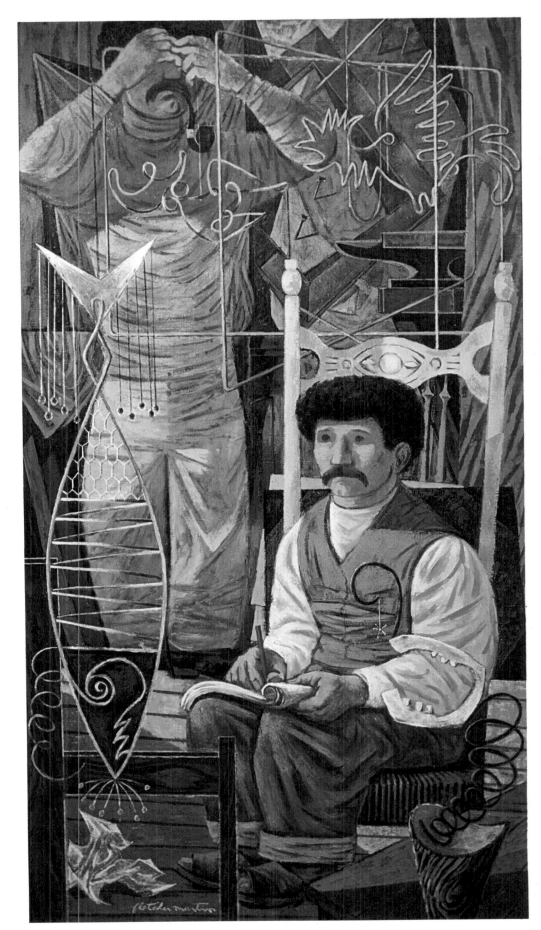

64. *Cherry Twice*. 1946.
Oil on canvas, 72 × 40".
The Whitney Museum of American Art,
New York

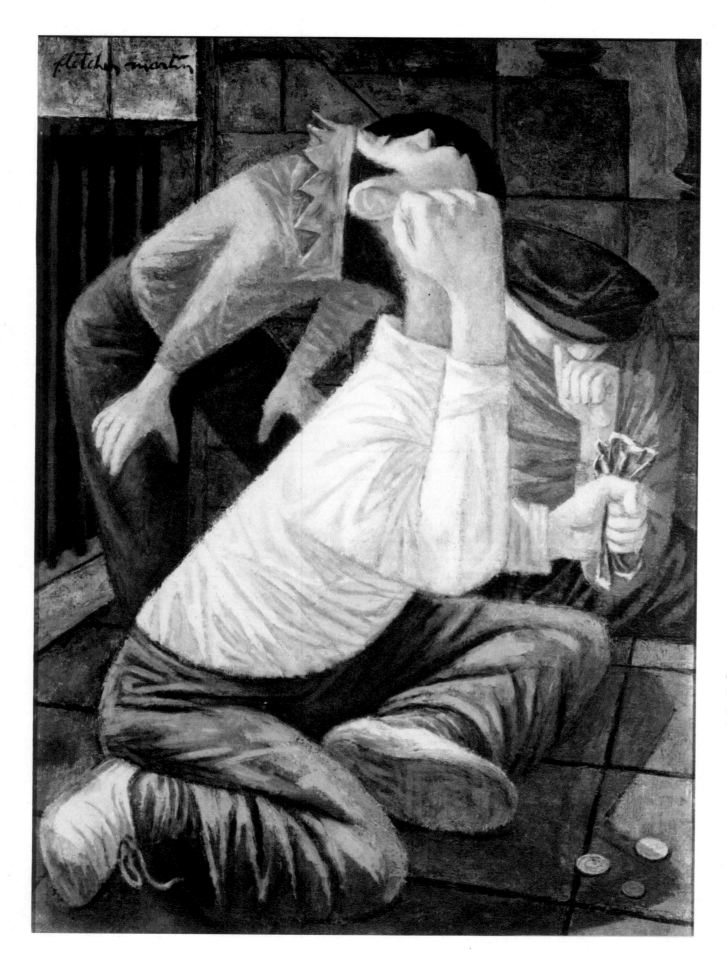

65.   *Urchin's Game.* 1946.
Oil on canvas, $30\frac{1}{2} \times 23''$.
Collection Sylvian Rittmaster Koehler,
Woodmere, N.Y.

66. *Eads Bridge from MacArthur Bridge.* 1946. Oil on canvas, 25 × 40″. University of Missouri at Columbia. Scruggs-Vandervoort-Barney Collection

67.   *Miners at the Coal Face*. 1948. Brush and reed and India ink, 13 × 19″. University of Pittsburgh Collections

68. *The Man Trip*. 1948.
Oil on canvas, 46 × 36″.
University of Pennsylvania,
Philadelphia

69. *Sylvia Sidney*. 1944–45. Oil on canvas, 60 × 30″.
Collection Sylvia Sidney, Roxbury, Conn.

70.   *Portrait of Charles Laughton as Captain Kidd.* 1945. Oil on canvas, 30 × 40″. Private collection

71. *Ritual*. 1946. Oil on canvas,
38 × 18″. Private collection

72.   *A Far-off City*. 1946. Oil on canvas, 26 × 44″. Private collection

73. *The Jungle*. 1948. Oil on canvas, 20×24″. Private collection

74.   *Victory*. 1949. Oil on canvas, 30×48″. Collection Mrs. Helen Martin, Los Angeles

75.   *The Undefeated.* 1949.
Oil on canvas, 52 × 24″.
Abbott Laboratories Art Collection,
Chicago

76. *The Glory.* 1949. Oil on canvas, 36 × 48″. Wichita State University Art Collection, Wichita, Kans.

77.   *The Barrier*. 1949. Oil on canvas, 40×60″. San Antonio Art League, Witte Memorial Museum, San Antonio, Texas

78. *Old Quarry*. 1949. Oil on canvas, 39 × 50″. Lowe Museum, University of Miami, Coral Gables, Fla.

79. *Summer Sea*. 1949.
Oil on canvas, 40×36″.
Private collection,
Sarasota, Fla.

80.   *The Blossom*. 1950. Oil on canvas, 24 × 36″. Private collection

81. *The Boat Basin*. 1951. Oil on canvas, 20 × 24″. Collection the artist

82. *The Toy Birds*. 1950. Oil on canvas, 46×28″.
Collection Carolyn Brown Negley, San Antonio, Texas

83. Study for *The Brothers*. 1951.
Pen and ink, 14×9¾″.
Addison Gallery of American Art,
Phillips Academy, Andover, Mass.

84. *Lamp and Skull*. 1950.
Oil on canvas, 34 × 14″.
Collection Mr. and Mrs. Heywood Hale Broun,
New York

85. *The Journey*. 1952.
Oil on canvas, 37×20″.
Collection Mrs. Lawrence Wood,
Refugio, Texas

86. *Sea Birds*. 1950. Oil on canvas, 24 × 30″. Private collection

87. *Running Birds*. 1951. Oil on board, 12 × 30". Collection Louis and Carolyn Sapir, New York

88. *Clown Act*. 1952.
Oil on canvas, 30 × 34".
Collection Bil Baird, New York

89. *Earth Machines*. 1951. Oil on canvas, 22×40″. Collection the artist

90. *Shooting Gallery*. 1952. Oil on canvas, 30×48″. Private collection

91. *Country Dance*. 1952.
Oil on canvas, 47 × 29″.
Collection Mr. and Mrs. John Stevenson,
New York

92. *Small Businessman*. 1953. Oil on canvas, 20 × 24″. Private collection

93. *Dancing Couple*. 1955.
Oil on canvas, 36 × 18″.
Collection Sam and Estelle Brouner,
Fort Lee, N.J.

94. *Figure with Fish Kite*. 1954.
Oil on canvas, 30 × 20″.
Collection Mr. and Mrs. Alexander E. Racolin,
Briarcliff Manor, N.Y.

95.   *Vacation.* 1953. Oil on canvas, 25 × 34″. Collection The Honorable and Mrs. William Benton, Southport, Conn.

96.   *The Sisters*. 1955.
Oil on canvas, $36 \times 24''$.
Private collection

97. *Memorable Day*. 1955.
Oil on canvas, 30 × 24″.
Private collection

98.   *Quarreling Gulls*. 1956. Oil on canvas, 16 × 36″. Private collection

99. *Whither Ulysses*. 1955.
Oil on canvas, 30×24″.
Private collection

100.   *Mother and Child with Hobby Horse*. 1955. Oil on canvas, 36×48″. Private collection

101. *Girl with Parasol.* 1955.
Oil on canvas, 28×20″.
Private collection

102. *Women Washing, Tepic.* 1956. Pen and India ink, 8×10″. Collection the artist

103. *Mourning at Noon*. 1957. Gouache, 13 × 19″. Collection Dr. and Mrs. Robert E. Rothenberg, New York

104.   *Mexican Village*. 1957. Casein on paper, 13 × 19″. Estate of Eve Loring

105. *La Turista*. 1957.
Oil on canvas, 36 × 24″.
Private collection

106. *Los Chicos*. 1957.
Oil on canvas, 54×44″.
Collection Mrs. Albert Dorne,
New York

107. *Las Mariposas*. 1957.
Oil on paper, 29×21″.
Collection Hal Findlay,
Alamos, Sonora, Mexico

108.   *Street Scene, Mazatlán.* 1956. Pen and ink, 9×12″.
Collection the artist

109.   *View of Guaymas.* 1956. Pen and ink, 8×10″.
Collection the artist

110.   *Mexican Landscape with Burros.* 1957. Oil on canvas, 28 × 36″. Collection Mr. and Mrs. Ira Wolfert, Lake Hill, N.Y.

111.   *Los Borrachos*. 1957. Oil on paper, 21 × 29″. Collection Mr. and Mrs. Charles F. Urschel, Jr., San Antonio, Texas

112.   *Mamacita*. 1957.
Oil on canvas, 30×20″.
Private collection

114. *Evening Nude*. 1957. Oil on canvas, 24×36″. Collection Mr. and Mrs. Elliot L. Gruenberg, West New York, N.J.

113. *Night Voices*. 1957. Oil on canvas, 40×40″.
National Academy of Design, New York. Permanent collection

115. *Child with Toy Bird.* 1958.
Oil on canvas, 37 × 20″.
Collection Mr. and Mrs. Clifford B. West,
Bloomfield Hills, Mich.

116.   *Las Criadas*. 1957. Oil on paper, 21 × 29″. Collection Mrs. Mason Letteau, Los Angeles

117. *Bullfight.* 1956. Oil on canvas, 32 × 42″. The Butler Institute of American Art, Youngstown, Ohio

118. *The Toss*. 1959.
Oil on canvas, 30 × 24″.
Collection Mr. and Mrs. Louis J. Buchman,
Loudonville, N.Y.

119. *The Wound.* 1959. Oil on canvas, 34×38″. Alma Walker Collection, Pebble Beach, Calif.

120.   *The Picador.* 1956. Casein on paper, 36×48″. Collection Mr. and Mrs. David A. Goodkind, Woodmere, N.Y.

121. *The Charge*. Detail of Plate 122

122. *The Charge*. 1965.
Oil on canvas, $48 \times 30\frac{1}{2}''$.
Collection Mr. and Mrs. Neil B. Lukow,
Merrick, N.Y.

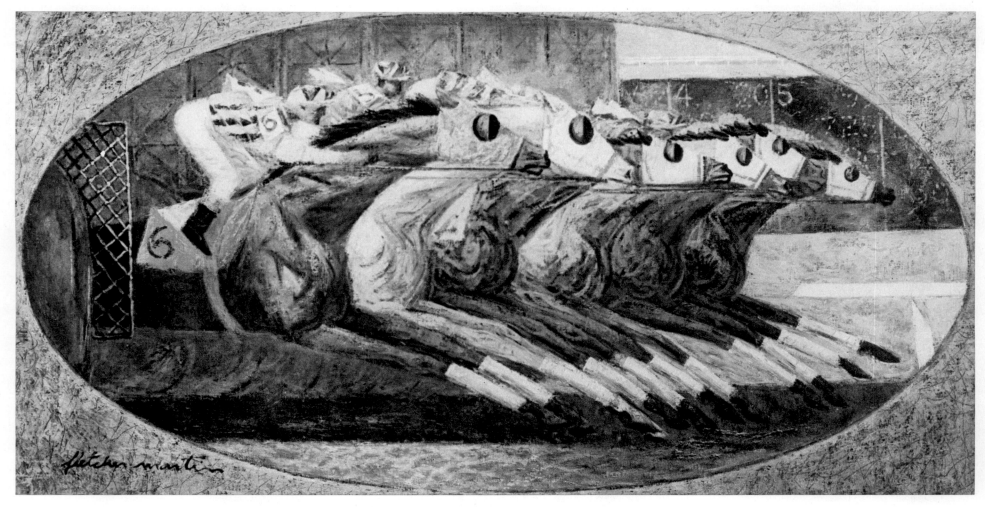

123. *Good at the Gate*. 1953. Oil on canvas, 20 × 40″. Collection Mrs. Joseph H. Forman, Woodstock, N.Y.

124. *Crowd Pleaser*. 1958. Oil on canvas, 20 × 30". Private collection

125. *Action at Second.* 1956.
Oil on canvas, 40 × 38″.
Collection Mr. and Mrs. Robert Rittmaster,
New York

126. *Friendly Game.* 1958.
Oil on canvas, 36 × 28″.
Collection Sylvian Rittmaster Koehler,
Woodmere, N.Y.

127. *The Corner*. 1962. Oil on canvas, 24×30″. Collection Mr. and Mrs. Sidney M. Brownstein, Woodmere, N.Y.

128. *Homage to Rocky Marciano*. 1969. Oil on canvas, 30×40″. Collection Stuart Rickseit

129. *February Picture*. 1956. Oil on canvas, 24 × 36″. Collection Mr. and Mrs. Lee Lebow, Coral Gables, Fla.

130.   *Sunday Morning*. 1956.
Oil on canvas, 30×25″.
Private collection

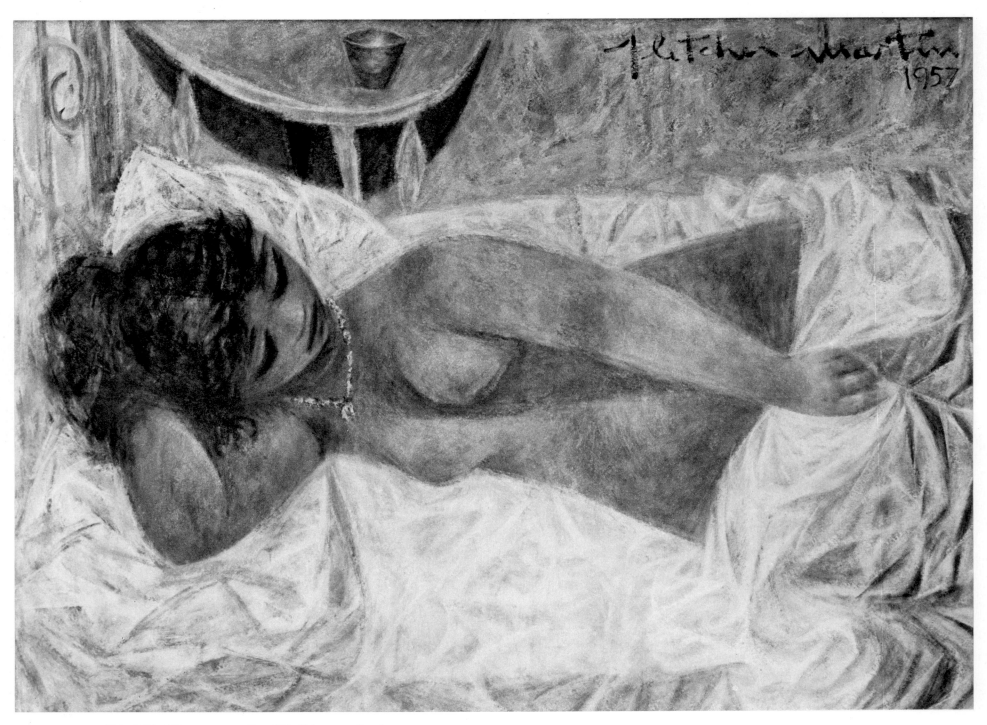

131. *Tarascan Girl.* 1957. Oil on paper, 21 × 29″. Private collection

132. *Pretty Rider*. 1958.
Oil on canvas, 34×18″.
Collection Dr. and Mrs. Arthur Sokoloff,
Coral Gables, Fla.

133. *The Flowering Tree*. 1957.
Oil on panel, 30 × 18″. Destroyed

134. *Newsstand.* 1957.
Oil on paper, 29×21″.
Collection Dr. and Mrs. Albert Tezla,
Duluth, Minn.

135. *Girl in Wicker Chair.* 1957.
Oil on canvas, 28×20″.
Private collection

136.   *Near the Sea*. 1957. Oil on canvas, 30×40″. Collection Mr. and Mrs. Irvin Goldberger, Hewlett Harbor, N.Y.

137. *Italian Girl*. 1959.
Casein on paper, 27×21″.
Roswell Museum and Art Center,
Roswell, N.M.

138.   *The White Village.* 1961. Oil on canvas, 30 × 50″. Collection Dr. and Mrs. Warren N. Swanson, Pacific Palisades, Calif.

139. *Nude with Tiger Cat.* 1959. Oil on mounted rag paper, 21 × 29″. Collection Donald B. Anderson, Roswell, N.M.

140. *Pretty Rider II*. 1960.
Casein on paper, 30×22″.
Private collection

141. *The Fountain.* 1963.
Pen and ink, $23 \times 17\frac{1}{2}''$.
Collection Peter Pollack,
Sarasota, Fla.

142. *The Capture*. 1962.
Acrylic on canvas, 40 × 30″.
Collection Mr. and Mrs. James Bond,
Philadelphia

143. *Child with Judas Figure.* 1962.
Acrylic on canvas, 28×22″.
Collection Jane and Hudson Walker,
New York

144. *The Gesture*. 1962.
Oil on canvas, 40 × 24″.
Collection Margaret M. Enoch,
New York

145.   Sketch for *Autumn Afternoon*. 1962.
Acrylic over pen on paper,
$19\frac{1}{2} \times 14\frac{1}{2}''$.
Collection Mr. and Mrs. Paul Anbinder,
Dobbs Ferry, N.Y.

146.   *The TV Watchers.* 1963. Oil on canvas, 24 × 36″. Collection Mr. and Mrs. George M. Simon, Albany, N.Y.

147. *Folk Song*. 1962.
Oil on canvas, 40 × 24″.
Collection Mr. and Mrs. Charles I. Rockmore,
New York

148. *The Waiting Wall.* 1962.
Oil on canvas, 29 × 20″.
Collection Margaret M. Enoch,
New York

149. *Lilith*. 1963.
Oil on canvas, 36×24″.
Collection Mr. and Mrs. James Bond,
Philadelphia

150.   *The Cigarette*. 1963. Oil on canvas, 22 × 32″. Private collection

151.   *Blonde in Black*. 1963. Acrylic on canvas, 22×40″. Private collection

152.   *The Street*. 1963. Acrylic on canvas, 28×28″.
Collection Sanford Smith, Hewlett, N.Y.

153.   *The Lovers II*. 1963. Oil on canvas, 17×37″. Private collection

154.   *Nude on Patterned Rug.* 1969. Pen and ink, 10 × 15″.
Collection the artist

155.   *By the Sea.* 1964. Oil on canvas, 36 × 24″.
Private collection

156. *Woman with Beads.* 1964.
Oil on canvas, 40×26″.
Collection Mr. and Mrs. Ira Wolfert,
Lake Hill, N.Y.

157. *Bather with Ball.* 1966. Charcoal, 24 × 17½″.
Collection Mr. and Mrs. James Mowry, Binghamton, N.Y.

158. *Jean Reading.* 1967. Pen and ink, 23½ × 18″.
Collection Andre P. Mele, Woodstock, N.Y.

159. *Seated Nude in Wrought ·
Iron Chair.* 1964. Oil on canvas,
30×24″. Collection
Mr. and Mrs. Arthur J. Levine,
Malverne, N.Y.

160. *O! Poor Parnassius.* 1965.
Oil on canvas, 28 × 23″.
Collection Elinor Jane Brickell,
Lawrence, N.Y.

161. *Opera Sketch, Don Pasquale.* 1965.
Pen and India ink, 24×18″.
Private collection

162. *Smiling Girl Reclining.* 1970.
Pen and ink, 19×23″.
Collection Mrs. Lester Cooke,
McLean, Va.

163. *Laughing Lancer*. 1967.
Pen and ink, 23 × 15″.
Collection Mr. and Mrs. Richard C. DeLuca,
Binghamton, N.Y.

164. *Woman in Orange Chair*. 1965.
Oil on canvas, 30×24″.
Collection Mr. and Mrs. Murray Strauss,
East Rockaway, N.Y.

165. *Women at the Window*. 1965.
Oil on canvas, 30×34″.
Collection Mr. and Mrs. Walter Spodek,
East Rockaway, N.Y.

166. *El Abrazo*. 1966.
Acrylic on paper, 22×17″.
Private collection

167. *Small Soldier*. 1966.
Oil on canvas, 30×20″.
Collection Mr. and Mrs. Castle W. Jordan,
Coral Gables, Fla.

168. *Sun Women*. 1966.
Oil on canvas, 37×27″.
Private collection

169.   *Between Poses*. 1966. Oil on canvas, 30×48″. Collection Mr. and Mrs. Jerome M. Wiesenthal

170. *William Bonney, Folk Hero*. 1964.
Oil on canvas, 40 × 20″
Collection Frank Leslie, Carefree, Ariz.

171. *Desert Village with Two Riders*. 1972.
Oil on Masonite, 40 × 30".
National Academy of Design, New York.
Permanent collection

172.   *The Capture III*. 1968.
Conté crayon, 40×24″.
Collection Mr. and Mrs. Eugene Gold,
New York

173.   *The Concert*. 1967.
Charcoal, 40×24″.
Collection Mr. and Mrs. Arthur Uffner,
Lawrence, N.Y.

174. *A Dish of Fish.* 1968. Oil on canvas, 15 × 24″. Collection Dr. F. M. Bayer

175. *Papaya with Butterfly*. 1966. Oil on canvas, 20 × 30″. Collection Mr. and Mrs. Arthur Uffner, Lawrence, N.Y.

176.   *In the Park*. 1968. Oil on canvas, 30×40″. Collection Mr. and Mrs. J. A. Melnick, Hewlett Bay Park, N.Y.

177. *Summer Song II*. 1968.
Acrylic on Masonite, 19×15″.
Private collection

178.   *The Cornucopia Kiss*. 1965. Oil on canvas, 48×48″. Estate of Eve Loring

179.   *The Betting Machine*. 1968. Oil on canvas, 30×40″. Collection Mr. and Mrs. Ronald E. Levick, Hewlett, N.Y.

180. *Rearing Horse.* 1970.
Pen and ink, 11 × 9″.
Collection the artist

181.   *Spring Meeting*. 1974. Oil on canvas, 18×36″. Collection the artist

182.   *Eight-Five-Three*. 1967–68. Oil on canvas, 24×52″. Collection Mr. and Mrs. Ira Rubin, Cedarhurst, N.Y.

183. *Bather with Towel*. 1968.
Oil on mounted rag paper, 24×17″.
Collection Dr. and Mrs. J. Gordon Rubin,
Saugerties, N.Y.

184.   *Girl with Guitar*. 1973. Oil on canvas, 20×26″. Private collection

185.	*The Whirligig*. 1967.
Oil on canvas, 30 × 24″.
Collection Mr. and Mrs. Seymour Perlman,
North Woodmere, N.Y.

186.	*Pretty Rider III*. 1968.
Oil on paper mounted on panel, 40 × 24″.
Collection Mr. and Mrs. Louis Weissman,
Lawrence, N.Y.

187.   *The Greek Girls*. 1968.
Oil on paper mounted on panel, $36 \times 24''$.
Collection Margaret M. Enoch, New York

188. *Irish Girl*. 1973.
Oil on canvas, 30×25″.
Private collection

189. *Alice Dreaming.* 1968.
Oil on canvas, 40 × 24″.
Collection Jean Arnold, Guanajuato, Mexico

190. *Fruit with Figure*. 1968. Oil on canvas, 24 × 30″. Private collection

191. *Grand Coulee Dam: The Left Bank*. 1970.
Watercolor, 29 × 35½″. Bureau of Reclamation,
US Department of the Interior, Washington, D.C.

192. *Grand Coulee Dam: High Scalers*. 1970.
Ink and watercolor, 29½ × 36½″. Bureau of Reclamation,
US Department of the Interior, Washington, D.C.

193. *Grand Coulee Dam: Penstocks and Piers*. 1972.
Watercolor, 29 × 37″. Bureau of Reclamation,
US Department of the Interior, Washington, D.C.

194. *Rim of Grand Coulee*. 1972.
Watercolor, 29 × 35½″. Bureau of Reclamation,
US Department of the Interior, Washington, D.C.

195. *Grand Coulee Spillway*. 1972. Oil on canvas, $32\frac{1}{2} \times 43\frac{1}{2}''$. Bureau of Reclamation, US Department of the Interior, Washington, D.C.

196. *Flame Pit, Kennedy Space Center.* 1970. Oil on canvas, 24 × 36″. NASA, Washington, D.C.

197. *The Hummingbird.* 1968.
Oil on canvas, 28 × 23″.
Collection Dr. and Mrs. Arthur Sokoloff,
Coral Gables, Fla.

198. *Mexican Kitchen Still Life*. 1973. Oil on canvas, 20 × 26″. Collection Mr. and Mrs. Herbert Alper, Hewlett Harbor, N.Y.

199. *The Parasol*. 1974.
Oil on canvas, 30 × 24″.
Collection Mr. and Mrs. Reagan Houston

200.   *The Sirens*. 1969.
Oil on canvas, 36×24″.
Private collection

201. *Girl with Yellow Fan*. 1970.
Oil on canvas, 30 × 20″.
Collection Mr. and Mrs. Bob Goldberg,
Cedarhurst, N.Y.

202. *The Matador*. 1973.
Oil on canvas, 40 × 26″.
Collection Mr. and Mrs. Harry S. Mayer,
Lawrence, N.Y.

BIOGRAPHICAL OUTLINE

1904 Born, Palisade, Colorado, son of Clinton H. and Josephine Martin. Father is a printer and editor of small-town newspapers.

1910 Family moves to Idaho and later to the state of Washington before returning to Idaho.

1920 Leaves home to live as migrant worker and hobo.

1922 Joins U.S. Navy.

1925 Marries Cecile Booth, established poetess and college classmate of his sister.

1926 Discharged from the Navy in San Francisco. Travels to Los Angeles. Begins working for Earl Hays, printer of motion picture inserts. Hays encourages Martin's interest in art.

1931 Works briefly with Foujita.

1932 Summers in New York City and Woodstock. Meets Yasuo Kuniyoshi, Alexander Brook, Louis Bouche, Peggy Bacon, Niles Spencer, and many other artists.

1933 Resumes work as a printer. Exhibits woodcuts, his first one-man show at Dalzell Hatfield Galleries, Los Angeles. Exhibits woodcuts at Scripps College, Claremont, California.

Assists David Alfaro Siqueiros, the Mexican painter, on a large fresco in Santa Monica, California. Becomes friendly with Philip Guston, Reuben Kadish, William Saroyan, Nathanael West, and Budd Schulberg.

1934 His first one-man exhibition of paintings at the San Diego Fine Arts Gallery.

1935 At the Sixteenth Annual Painters and Sculptors Exhibition at the Los Angeles County Museum *Rural Family* earns the $500 Van Rensselaer Wilbur Prize and the First Los Angeles County Museum Award.

Has one-man exhibition at the Los Angeles County Museum.

Marries Henriette Lichtenstein, a movie scriptwriter.

1936 Leaves Hays to work full time on large frescoes (since destroyed) in North Hollywood High School's auditorium, a WPA Art Project.

One-man exhibition at Howard Putzel Gallery, Hollywood.

One-man show at Jake Zeitlin Gallery, Los Angeles.

1937 Wins $4900 Award from U.S. Section of Fine Arts competition for a mural in the Federal Building, San Pedro, California.

1938 Designs three bas-relief sculpture panels for the Boundary County Courthouse, Bonners Ferry, Idaho.

Begins two-year position teaching drawing at the Art Center School, Los Angeles.

1939 Museum of Modern Art, New York, purchases *Trouble in Frisco* for its permanent collection.

A Lad from the Fleet earns the Second Los Angeles County Museum Award.

One-man exhibition at Los Angeles County Museum.

Paints mural for the Post Office, La Mesa, Texas.

Exhibits watercolors at the All-California show at the Riverside Museum, New York.

1940 Joins Hudson Walker Gallery in New York.

Later joins Midtown Galleries in New York where his first New York one-man exhibition takes place.

Succeeds Grant Wood as Artist-in-Residence at State University, Iowa City, Iowa.

One-man exhibition at the University Gallery.

Paints mural for the Post Office, Kellogg, Idaho.

Executes twelve panels for the Ada County Courthouse, Boise, Idaho. Project never completed.

Metropolitan Museum of Art, New York, purchases *Juliet*.

1941   Succeeds Thomas Hart Benton as head of the Department of Painting at Kansas City Art Institute.

One-man exhibition at the Iowa Union.

Divorced from Henriette Lichtenstein.

Marries Maxine Ferris, a nurse.

1942   One-man show at the William Rockhill Nelson Gallery and Atkins Museum of Fine Arts, Kansas City.

1943   Accepts assignment from *Life* to work in North Africa as artist-war correspondent. Reproductions in the Christmas issue spread Martin's reputation.

1944   One-man exhibition of war sketches and paintings at Midtown Galleries, New York.

Illustrates *Tales of the Gold Rush* by Bret Harte for The Limited Editions Club.

Accepts another assignment from *Life* to document conditions in London and Normandy.

Joins Associated American Artists.

Travels to Hollywood to paint portraits of Charles Laughton, Yvonne de Carlo, and Sylvia Sidney for *Life*.

1945   Returns to New York. Executes a series of cityscapes for the Nathan M. Ohrbach Collection.

Accepts commission from *Sports Illustrated* to document the second Rocky Marciano-Ezzard Charles fight.

Divorced from Maxine Ferris.

1946   Illustrates *Mutiny on the Bounty* by Nordhoff and Hall for The Limited Editions Club.

Marries Helen Donovan.

Accepts commission to paint scenes of the rivers of Missouri for the Scruggs-Vandervoort-Barney Collection.

Accepts commission to document highway construction in New York for *The Lamp*, the company magazine of Standard Oil.

Moves to Woodstock, New York.

1947   *Dancer Dressing* awarded the Walter Lippincott Prize at the Pennsylvania Academy of Fine Arts.

Builds residence and studio on Overlook Mountain in Woodstock.

Begins a two-year teaching position at the Art Students League, Woodstock.

Accepts assignment from the Gimbel-Pennsylvania Art Collection to paint a series describing anthracite mining in Wilkes Barre, Pennsylvania.

1948   One-man exhibition at the Associated American Artists, New York.

Accepts commission from *Fortune* magazine to document the production of newsprint.

1949   *Cherry Twice* awarded the Altman Prize by the National Academy of Design.

Accepts commission to paint scenes of tobacco production in North Carolina for the Lucky Strike Cigarette Company.

Begins a two-year residency at the University of Florida, Gainesville.

Retrospective exhibition of paintings at the University Gallery.

1950   Accepts commission from Abbott Laboratories to prepare a portfolio on native health conditions in the Northwest and Alaska and among thirteen Indian reservations.

1951   Wins Merit Award of the Art Directors Club of Chicago.

Accepts position of Visiting Artist for the summer session of Claremont College, Claremont, California, which assembles a one-man exhibition.

1952   Joins faculty of the Albany Institute of History and Art.

Visiting Artist during the summer session of Mills College, Oakland, California.

One-man exhibition at Associated American Artists, New York.

1953   Receives Gold Medal of the Art Directors Club of Philadelphia.

1954   *Figure with Fish Kite* awarded the Clark Prize by the National Academy of Design.

Fletcher Martin, written by Barbara Ebersole and William Saroyan, published by the University of Florida Press.

Joins John Heller Gallery, New York.

Visiting Artist during the summer session of the University of Minnesota at Duluth.

Retrospective exhibition held by the Tweed Museum of Art, University of Minnesota, Duluth.

Joins the guiding faculty, Famous Artists School, Westport, Connecticut.

1955   Visiting Artist during the summer session of the Castle Hill Foundation, Ipswich, Massachusetts.

Receives Gold Medal of the Art Directors Club of New York.

One-man exhibition at the John Heller Gallery, New York.

1956   One-man show at the Francis Lynch Gallery, Los Angeles.

Visiting Artist at Northern Michigan College, Marquette.

1957   Executes portfolio of western Mexican coastal sites for *Home and Highway*, the company magazine of Allstate Insurance.

Visiting Artist during the summer session of the University of Minnesota, Duluth.

Conducts spring workshop at the San Antonio Art Institute.

1958   Again conducts workshop at the San Antonio Art Institute.

One-man exhibition at the Witte Memorial Museum, San Antonio.

Visiting Artist at the Huntington Galleries, Huntington, West Virginia.

Accepts appointment to head the Department of Drawing, Los Angeles County Art Institute.

Guides a group of art students through Europe.

1959   Travels with a group of students through Mexico.

Conducts winter workshop in drawing at the State University of New York at New Paltz.

1960   Visiting Artist at Washington State University's extension in Spokane.

One-man exhibition at the Cheney Cowles Museum, Spokane.

Illustrates Jack London's *The Sea Wolf* for The Limited Editions Club.

One-man show of drawings at the University of Maine, Orono.

1961   Spends winter and spring in Yucatan and Quintana Roo, Mexico.

Conducts workshop again at Washington State University, Spokane.

Divorced from Helen Donovan.

1963   One-man exhibition at Milch Galleries, New York. Paints and travels through Mexico.

Conducts workshop at Rochester Art Center, Rochester, Minnesota, where he has one-man show.

1964   Receives Ford Foundation–American Federation of Art Grant, to be Artist-in-Residence at Roswell Museum and Art Center, Roswell, New Mexico.

One-man exhibition at Roswell Museum.

Marries Jean Small, novelist and playwright.

1965   Illustrates Upton Sinclair's *The Jungle* for The Limited Editions Club.

Conducts summer workshop at the Huntington Galleries, Huntington, West Virginia.

One-man show at the Huntington Galleries.

Teaches and exhibits at the University of Bridgeport where he becomes the second Albert Dorne Professor of Drawing.

1966   Participates in exhibition touring England, France, Italy, South Africa, and Central and South America.

Teaches at the Art Students League, Woodstock, New York.

1967   Begins a year as Artist-in-Residence at the Roberson Center for the Arts and Sciences, Binghamton, New York.

1968   Retrospective at the Roberson Center.

1969   Becomes Associate of the National Academy of Design. Accepts commission from NASA to document the launching of Apollo 13 from Cape Kennedy.

1970   Accepts assignment from the Bureau of Reclamation to paint scenes of various western dam sites.

Moves to Mexico for an indefinite period.

1972   Accepts assignment from the Bureau of Reclamation to fully document Grand Coulee Dam.

1973   Becomes National Academician of the National Academy of Design.

1975   Accepts assignment from NASA to document launch of Apollo-Soyuz test and Viking probe preparation at Cape Kennedy.

BIBLIOGRAPHY

BOOKS

Cheney, Sheldon. *The Story of Modern Art.* Mid-Century rev. ed. New York: Viking Press, 1958.

Ebersole, Barbara. *Fletcher Martin.* Foreword by William Saroyan. Gainesville: University of Florida Press, 1954.

Green, Samuel M. *American Art: A Historical Survey.* New York: Ronald Press Co., 1966.

Guitar, Mary Anne. *The 22 Famous Painters and Illustrators Tell How They Work.* New York: David McKay Co., 1964.

Larkin, Oliver. *Art and Life in America.* New York: Rinehart & Company, 1949.

ARTICLES

"Andrew Carnegie: His Millions Made from Pittsburgh Steel Put on Greatest Shows of Art by Living Artists." *Life,* vol. 16, no. 17 (April 24, 1944), pp. 74–79.

"Benton Ousted." *Art Digest,* vol. 15, no. 16 (May 15, 1941), p. 14.

"The Blackfeet, the Makah, the Tlinket Indians, and the Eskimo of Alaska." *Abbott Laboratories Magazine,* vol. 147, no. 6 (June, 1950), pp. 16–24.

Boswell, Peyton. "Fletcher Martin, Painter of Memories." *Parnassus,* vol. 12, no. 6 (October, 1940), pp. 6–13.

———— "Fletcher Martin Paints the War in Africa." *Art Digest,* vol. 18, no. 7 (January 1, 1944), p. 8.

———— "*Life* Visits Fletcher Martin." *Art Digest,* vol. 15, no. 4 (November 15, 1940), p. 3.

Campbell, Lawrence. "Odyssey of a Shellback." *Art Students League News,* vol. 3, no. 13 (August 1, 1950), pp. 14–18.

"Charles Laughton in the Movie 'Captain Kidd' Painted by Fletcher Martin." *Life,* vol. 19, no. 19 (November 5, 1945), p. 62.

Coates, Robert, "The Art Galleries." *The New Yorker,* vol. 16, no. 41 (November 23, 1940), pp. 59–60.

Cook, Ted. "Fletcher Martin." *California Arts and Architecture,* vol. 57, no. 8 (September, 1940), pp. 16–17.

Day, Worden. "Fletcher Martin Exhibition at Milch Gallery." *Art News,* vol. 62, no. 2 (April 1, 1963), p. 54.

"Defense Painting: *Life* Recruits Major Artists." *Life,* vol. 11, no. 1 (July 7, 1941), pp. 60–64.

"Exhibition at Midtown Galleries." *Art News,* vol. 42, no. 16 (January 1, 1944), p. 30.

"Exhibition of Paintings and Drawings of Mexico at Heller Gallery." *Arts,* vol. 32, no. 2 (November, 1957), p. 51.

"Figure Studies and Landscapes at Associated American Artists." *Art News,* vol. 47, no. 7 (November 1, 1948), p. 46.

"Fletcher Martin." *Art Digest,* vol. 20, no. 4 (November 15, 1945), p. 22.

"Fletcher Martin." *Art Digest,* vol. 26, no. 14 (April 15, 1952), p. 17.

"Fletcher Martin." *Famous Artists Magazine,* vol. 2, no. 3 (Spring 1954), pp. 6–9.

"Fletcher Martin: Some Drawings Made on the African Front." *American Artist Magazine,* vol. 8, no. 3 (March 1, 1944), pp. 13–16.

"Fletcher Martin Illustrates John Steinbeck." *Famous Artists Magazine,* vol. 19, no. 1 (January, 1971), pp. 12–17.

"Fletcher Martin on the West Coast." *Art Digest,* vol. 18, no. 20 (September 1, 1944), p. 12.

"Fletcher Martin Replaces Benton." *Parnassus,* vol. 13, no. 5 (May, 1941), p. 191.

"Fletcher Martin Replaces Benton in Kansas City." *Art News,* vol. 40, no. 7 (May 15, 1941), p. 7.

George, Laverne. "Exhibition at the Heller Gallery." *Arts,* vol. 30, no. 2 (November, 1955), p. 54.

Guitar, Mary Anne. "Close-Up of the Artist Fletcher Martin." *Famous Artists Magazine,* vol. 11, no. 2 (Winter 1962), pp. 16–19.

Kent, Norman. "Fletcher Martin—A Rugged American Artist." *American Artist Magazine,* vol. 11, no. 10 (December, 1947), pp. 14–21.

Lane, James W. "Fletcher Martin." *Art News,* vol. 40, no. 8 (June 1, 1941), p. 30.

"LeRoy Buys Martin." *Art Digest,* vol. 15, no. 20 (September 1, 1941), p. 6.

"*Life* Artist Sketches the St. Lô Sector During Lull Before Battle." *Life,* vol. 17, no. 6 (August 7, 1944), pp. 22–23.

Martin, Fletcher. "Composition." *The Art of the Artist: Theory and Techniques of Art by the Artists Themselves.* New York: Crown Publishers, 1951.

——— "The Eye Is Your Camera." *Famous Artists Magazine,* vol. 6, no. 2 (Winter 1957), pp. 6–10.

——— "Statement Concerning Illustrating *The Sea Wolf.*" The Limited Editions Club *Monthly Letter,* no. 333 (August, 1961), pp. 7–8.

"Martin Married in Mexico." *Art Digest,* vol. 15, no. 20 (September 1, 1941), p. 6.

"Martin—Painter, Printer, Proletarian—Wins Los Angeles Prize." *Art Digest,* vol. 9, no. 17 (June 1, 1935), p. 7.

"Martin Scores." *Art Digest,* vol. 14, no. 7 (January 1, 1940), p. 14.

McBride, Henry. "That Modern Problem." *Art News,* vol. 51, no. 3 (May 1, 1952), p. 48.

"Meet Mr. Martin." *Art Digest,* vol. 16, no. 2 (October 15, 1941), p. 20.

"Millier Thrilled." *Art Digest,* vol. 14, no. 6 (December 15, 1939), p. 26.

"New York Introduced to Fletcher Martin." *Art Digest,* vol. 15, no. 4 (November 15, 1940), p. 6.

"New York Sees Fletcher Martin Drawings." *Art Digest,* vol. 15, no. 17 (June 1, 1941), p. 21.

"Normandy." *Life,* vol. 18, no. 18 (April 30, 1945), p. 42.

"North Africa: Rear." *Life,* vol. 15, no. 26 (December 27, 1943), Cover, pp. 60–67.

O'Hara, Frank. "Exhibition at the Heller Gallery." *Art News,* vol. 54, no. 7 (November 1, 1955), p. 50.

"Original Christmas Cards." *Art In America,* vol. 52, no. 6 (December, 1964), pp. 97–99.

Pearson, Ralph M. "Pictures in *Life* Magazine." *Art Digest,* vol. 19, no. 17 (June 1, 1945), p. 22.

"A Portfolio of Sketches." *Florida Anthropologist,* vol. 3, nos. 3–4 (November, 1950), pp. 9–11, 7–9.

Salpeter, Harry. "The Middleweight Artist." *Esquire,* vol. 17, no. 5 (May, 1942), p. 88.

Saroyan, William. "Fletcher Martin." *Art Digest,* vol. 29, no. 3 (November 1, 1954), pp. 10–11.

Seckler, Dorothy Gees. "Fletcher Martin Paints a Mother and *Famous Artists Magazine,* vol. 3, no. 3 (Spring 1955), p. 14.

"Speaking of Pictures . . . This Is Mural America for Rural Americans." *Life,* vol. 17, no. 23 (December 4, 1939), pp. 12–13.

"Sylvia Sidney, An Oil Painting by Fletcher Martin." *Life,* vol. 19, no. 11 (September 10, 1945), p. 61.

Taylor, Rex. "Fletcher Martin: Sports King of the Art World." *Famous Artists Magazine,* vol. 5, no. 1 (Autumn 1956), pp. 13–15.

"Teacher's Show." *Time,* vol. 36, no. 22 (November 25, 1940), p. 60.

"Yvonne de Carlo, A Painting by Fletcher Martin." *Life,* vol. 19, no. 26 (December 24, 1945), p. 65.

EXHIBITION CATALOGUES (IN CHRONOLOGICAL ORDER)

Los Angeles. Dalzell Hatfield Galleries. *The Woodcuts of Fletcher Martin.* Commentary by Merle Armitage. 1933.

Los Angeles. Los Angeles County Museum. *The Sixteenth Annual Exhibition of Painters and Sculptors.* April 25–June 6, 1935.

Colorado Springs. Colorado Springs Fine Arts Center. *The Fourth Annual Exhibition of Paintings by Artists West of the Mississippi.* 1938.

Los Angeles. Los Angeles County Museum. *Fletcher Martin.* December, 1939.

San Francisco. Golden Gate International Exposition, Department of Fine Arts. *Contemporary Art.* 1939.

New York. Midtown Galleries. *Fletcher Martin: Exhibition of Paintings.* Foreword by Peyton Boswell. November 11–30, 1940.

Iowa City. Iowa Union. *Emil Ganso and Fletcher Martin.* March, 1941.

Philadelphia. Philadelphia Art Alliance. *Fighting Art.* January 17–February 20, 1944.

Hagerstown. Washington County Museum of Fine Arts. *American Paintings Today.* Foreword by John Richard Croft. April 1–29, 1945.

New York. Associated American Artists. *Fletcher Martin.* October 25–November 14, 1948.

Gainesville. University of Florida. *First Annual Exhibition of the Florida Art Group on National Circuit.* May, 1950–April, 1951.

Gainesville. University of Florida. *Second Annual Exhibition of the Florida Art Group on National Circuit.* May, 1951–April, 1952.

New York. Associated American Artists. *Fletcher Martin—Recent Works.* March 31–April 19, 1952.

Albany. Albany Institute of History and Art. *Fletcher Martin—Paintings and Drawings.* October 19–November 1, 1952.

Duluth. Tweed Museum of Art, University of Minnesota. *A Retrospective Exhibition of the Work of Fletcher Martin.* May 2–31, 1954.

New York. John Heller Gallery. *Fletcher Martin.* October 25–November 12, 1955.

Los Angeles. Francis Lynch Gallery. *Fletcher Martin.* 1956.

Pomona. Los Angeles County Fair Association. *Contemporary Arts of the United States.* September 14–30, 1956.

Duluth. Tweed Museum of Art, University of Minnesota. *Fletcher Martin in Mexico.* April 28–May 31, 1957.

San Antonio. Witte Memorial Museum. *Fletcher Martin: Exhibition of Paintings and Drawings.* January 26–February 9, 1958.

Dallas. NYE Galleries. *Fletcher Martin—Paintings—Drawings.* May 5–23, 1958.

Orono. Carnegie Hall Gallery. University of Maine. *Fletcher Martin—*

Drawings. December, 1960.

Spokane. Cheney Cowles Memorial Museum. *Fletcher Martin.* June 15–August 1, 1961.

Norfolk. Norfolk Museum of Arts and Sciences. *XXth American Drawing Annual.* January 7–27, 1963.

New York. Milch Galleries. *Fletcher Martin—Recent Paintings.* March 26–April 13, 1963.

Scottsdale. Gallery of Modern Art. *Opening Exhibition.* 1963.

Rochester. Rochester Art Center. *Fletcher Martin: Exhibition of Paintings, Drawings, and Prints.* July, 1963.

Roswell. Roswell Museum and Art Center. *Paintings by Fletcher Martin.* February 16–March 16, 1964.

Youngstown. Butler Institute of American Art. *29th Annual Midyear Show.* July 5–September 7, 1964.

Binghamton. Roberson Center for the Arts and Sciences. *Fletcher Martin: A Thirty Year Retrospective.* Commentary by Fletcher Martin. 1968.

INDEX

Asterisks (*) denote colorplates

PHOTOCREDITS

Colten Photos, New York: 63, 67, 72, 73, 75, 76, 79, 86; Peter Jones: 1; Peter A. Juley & Son, New York: 31, 50, 57, 62, 71, 81, 84, 87, 89, 123, 174, 176, 187; John D. Murray: 83; O. E. Nelson, New York: 112, 120; Patteson, San Antonio, Texas: 171, 181, 184, 199, 202; Phoenix Photos, Woodstock, N.Y.: 138, 150; Eric Pollitzer, New York: 2, 11, 13, 17, 27, 33, 36, 42, 43, 51, 61, 64, 65, 68, 77, 78, 88, 95, 102, 103, 106, 110, 113, 114, 117, 118, 121, 122, 125, 129, 136, 140, 141, 146–48, 157–60, 163, 164, 166, 168–70, 172, 173, 175, 182, 185, 188, 189, 197, 198, 200; John D. Schiff, New York: 92, 98–100; Robert Sewall, Woodstock, N.Y.: 111, 116, 130, 131, 134; Robert Singhaus, Carmel, Calif.: 119